RAYMOND WHO?

AN AUTOBIOGRAPHY

BY

RAYMOND FROGGATT

SCALA MUSIC

Designed,Typeset and Produced by
The Thumbprint Partnership, Shropshire, England.
Illustrations & Cartoons by L. Wassell.

Typeset in Times 10/11pt.

Printed and bound in Great Britain.

TO LOUISE

He who steals my purse
Steals trash
But he who robs me of my good name
Leaves me poor indeed.

William Shakespeare

ACKNOWLEDGEMENTS

I will offer my warm thanks to the following people for their invaluable assistance in my dealings with life. Also for their unfailing loyalty at all times.

H. Cain, Lou Clark, Len Ablethorpe, for their time and teachings, their understanding and playing of my songs; Stuart and Patsy Reid my Publishers and good friends, Terry Kennedy for his love of my music, Pat McCormick for typing and correcting my dreadful spelling and punctuation; my mother for having me and calming my wrath in times of tension; my many thousands of fans who share their love with me; my enemies for giving me strength to defeat them;
Roger Browne, Bruce Caulkin, Tom Farnell, H. & Lynn Cain for being wings on my heels.

Raymond Froggatt

CONTENTS

FOREWORD

RAYMOND FROGGATT, whom I have known for over twenty-five years, asked me to write an introduction for his book.

I must say that I felt delighted that he should have chosen me for the task. When I look back over the years I remember well our first meeting. Here was a young man so positive of the road he was about to take, having no thought of the dangers and the disappointments that could and would exist. Here he was, with his group, ready to take on the music world. He was the one who had the courage and determination that is essential to survive in the crazy world of show business, and he has proved it by his success over this long period.

Needless to say, in such a business there have been times when only the pure guts of this man made it possible. His task was not just to succeed for himself but the maintenance of his group, who depended on him. This I can say, that never once did he not make this his major duty and this concern for his musicians has brought him the loyalty that he so rightly merits.

He was, and is, a writer of great songs and though he himself has not crowned his career to date with an international hit, his song

STUART REID

writing has brought him successes through artists such as Cliff Richard, Dave Clark, and on the Continent such favourites as Marie La Foret.

His gut belief has taken him to gamble at great lengths that seemed at the time impossible, like his staging of his group and himself by the Birmingham Philharmonic Orchestra backing. It was an amazing success, which brought him accolades from all the musical papers and press.

This man is forever reaching out to surpass every previous effort, and in every endeavour has achieved his goal.

I must, just for a moment make mention of one person who from day one has helped and inspired Raymond in all his ventures. His great friend and guitarist Hartley Cain. When you have a friend of the character of this man you are most fortunate indeed.

Raymond has a tremendous feel for the musical theatre, but even stronger is his love affair with his audience and I have seen the effect this has - IT'S MAGIC.

When you consider that this man has been touring England on and off for twenty years, and still fills theatres wherever he plays, his fan mail is so large you would think he had just had an enormous record hit yesterday. As you can imagine, this man is forever searching greater musical projects. His insatiable urge drives him on to further heights. You, being fans, must already know that your star is to play in the most famous theatre, the LONDON PALLADIUM. I am sure that this show will be another triumph for this wonderful artiste.

You no doubt by this time must be thinking that such praise is, to say the least, an exaggeration. Of his talents - no - but he is still just a human being with all his faults.

His story has not ended, for I believe he has more pinnacles to climb ...

Stuart Reid,
Froggie's Music Publisher for 25 years

Chapter one

BIRTH OF A DREAM

I suppose the reasons for writing this account of my life since becoming a runner in that classic race called 'the music industry', are simply my natural ego, which demands I should be loved and admired by all my fellow human beings. Also the fear that my contributions, achievements, failures, loves and hates could all pass by without notice.

It might seem like foolish dreaming if I were to hope that this story would be of

interest to a public that generally keeps its reading hours exclusively for the pursuit of eavesdropping into the life of someone who has already found the

dizzy heights of fame and riches. How then, could this same public find interest in these pages, which portray the humble beginnings of a music band that remains, up until the day of writing, ever still humbly beginning.

It may be that writing a book is like writing a song. You never know - it might appeal to somebody, and it could be a hit! So write on foolish dreamer.

How to begin? Yes, it's like a song. How to construct? So very like a song. Automatically, I feel I should start at the birth of my band, which in many ways now feels like the birth of myself. The Birmingham streets were my mother's womb, the musicians my brothers, my mistakes were by teachers, my audience has been my judge - sometimes a lenient, understanding judge and sometimes a cruel hanging judge; but always a judge I knew well.

It will be important for you to see the people I know through my eyes, so that you might seem them as I do, and maybe capture their beauty, or sense their talent, perceive their ugliness, treachery or loyalty. I have reached out to these people in blindness, my vision narrowed and blurred

by my dreams. The dreams I thought they could all see. In my ignorance I failed to understand or imagine that they too have their own ideas of future happiness. Their stars to be chased, just as real and romantic as mine could ever be.

My professional heart has not been divorced from my personal life, thus causing strange chills among friends who in their innocent misunderstanding, find me difficult to measure. You cannot wear a dream as a cloak to be admired, for dreams do not make men and men do not make dreams. They are just there - pieces of hope scattered everywhere, for everyone. You damned dream! You beautiful dream! You brought me such warm friendship, such cursed pain, kindness and tears, that when cried they gave me an inner glow of intense, sad pleasure, that they could have formed a sea before I would wish them to cease.

This music industry is littered with casualties of bad management, rotten records, naive self-representation, drugs, booze and plain trickery. I am no exception to these, when having found myself victim of these accepted booby traps I told myself 'I am at school here, I am learning my trade'. I could not afford to wallow in self-pity - the glorified image of the ruined great artiste was not for me. I have a band to think of. We rely on each other. We are the only ones who care. We are the only ones who believe that what we are doing is good. We will make it, we are certain of that. We are certainly certain of that, aren't we?

It seems a lifetime since I began this journey, there has always been one wall or another to climb and I'm sure these walls made everything a lot more interesting. It's true that dreams have thorns (except for the artificial kind) so at least we are getting scratched and irritated by the real thing.

At nineteen years of age I had nothing very much to say about anything. The usual adolescent existence of confusion, pigheadedness, and the joining of the pack. Together we knew every answer; alone, we had only questions. Among that noisy, confident, youthful bunch there were a few friends, here's one, and he's gone now, dear friend, do you remember the days a few years back when we stood as one and the world couldn't break us? We sat in bars and drank ourselves stupid. We both agreed that we didn't need anything and we laughed at the warning 'one day we'd get older'.

The world of that homespun picture we lived in, painted not by experience - only things we believed in. The only colour that was true, is that I really loved you.

In ten short years to have been best man at your wedding; godfather to your first child, and then to carry you to your grave, was really pushing friendship at bit far; but you never did take anything very serious, did you?

It's strange the way different sorts of pain hurt in different sorts of ways. For instance, the pain of losing a friend to death seems a hopeless, empty and angry hurt that is both painless and futile, and yet it's a pain that leaves one feeling almost safe and complacent. On the other hand the sheer distress and loneliness of physical pain is so cruelly threatening that in its danger one can feel positively abandoned. The latter of these two ills was to strike at my life first whilst I thought more or less nothing but a black eye could cause pain. This was to teach me how painless a black eye could be.

'So odd, this dull ache', thought the eighteen year old tough guy. Odd indeed, it would not pass. He had not sweated in the night and felt cold

ALL ENQUIRIES :-
GAZETTE ENTERTAINMENTS
021 - 236 5610

RAYMOND FROGGATT

FAN CLUB :- EDWIN H. MORRIS
15. 17. ST. GEORGE STREET
LONDON W.1.

before. Something inside him was very wrong. Then the terrible almost unbearable eruption of hurt the visual horror; the flood of urinated clotted black blood, final proof that his life was surely falling away as he watched. It turned out to be tuberculosis of the kidneys and bladder. Not as romantic as someone going gradually blind with a brain tumour, but I can assure you, just as deadly and incredibly painful.

This episode in my life proved to be quite time consuming and laid me low for some two years. How much these years taught me. If only we could all have time to think about people and witness pure love and affection without any strings attached. I realised that our petty little differences are so selfish and stupid. I found that no one belongs to anybody and we owe each other nothing but each other. How ridiculous our acted moments of self-pity, so that someone we think we own will respond in some favourable way. I suppose I

was changing. I was beginning to see myself and others in such a different way. I saw a real purpose for being here.

I never wanted to be close to anyone. I had seen misfortune as funny; loyalty as weakness; loudness as bravery; cunning as cleverness, and love as stupidity. Strangely, I didn't pray, I couldn't see God then, and the world was still a stranger to me. I wanted to contribute to give something of myself to these new thoughts. I wanted to try to help people to see their own feelings by relating to them my own.

I hadn't learnt my trade then but I knew instinctively that my work must never seem personal. They must see themselves through my songs. What a wonderful feeling it was, not knowing if I was going to be any good; but I had a true reason to try to reach people.

Thus was born the beginning of my dream. I had written lots of words which I laughingly called songs or poems. I was like everyone else who starts to write. The themes were of death, rivers, lost love, trees or war. All noble subjects indeed, but perhaps a little heavy for the pen of this inexperienced minstrel. I found myself trapped in my emotions and sounding rather silly. I needed help, comrades, fellow dreamers, people to play my songs to. I wanted a band.

I had been out of hospital for about three weeks, following eighteen months of treatment to rid my unfortunate organs of the dreaded disease. Sadly, this unprovoked minute attacker had killed one of my innocent and hardworking kidneys stone dead. A kidney whose only crime had been to filter the system of an over-indulgent, lunatic, drunken youth. This dead, offending, innocent victim had now to be plucked from my body just as soon as a bed became available in Dudley Road Hospital, unfairly known locally as 'The Slaughterhouse'.

This interlude in my treatment gave me time to look for my so-needed Band of Players.

It was suggested to me by a friend, who had the sort of kindness that really helps, that I should advertise in the local press. I don't suppose he realises that he changed my life with that advice, but I remain to this day extremely grateful to him. He is Derek Cooper, a young man who never gave me the impression that he was tolerating me, or tolerating what must have seemed to him to be rather silly idea.

I have always been very sensitive and perceptive to the type of people who have their 'favourites', those who consider others to be only worth their tolerance. They bask in each other's company, discussing how stupid some poor unfortunate people are because they don't look at an official form with the same self-opinionated, greedy interest as they do, and so are less likely to grasp what it means right away. When these 'perfect' people decide one day that they will pour some of their pompous garbage over someone whom they consider stupid, and in need of their marvellous guidance, find that they get a reaction to which they are extremely shocked, and inevitably retreat to their 'favourites', to lament with each other as to how anyone can treat them this way, when they have only the interest of the stupid at heart. Dear Derek is not one of these . He is a very helpful and kind human being. Thanks pal!

Frog with his mom Lucy, shortly before she died.

Chapter two

THE BAND

'Musicians needed to back singer for new Night Club opening shortly. Regular work. Must be professionals. Please ring .....'

The advert caused the 'phone to ring for a whole week, with what seemed like hundreds of out-of-work players, or bands, needing a singer. I auditioned them at a private house of a friend of mine. It was during that week I realised how little I knew about musicians and what made them tick.

A lot of these players seemed too good for me, and some of them I didn't like personally. I'm sure a great deal of them didn't like me either! After a few days I was getting nowhere, and wasn't looking forward to the arrival of the next lot of players.

Then it happened. The entrance of three people who were to become some of the dearest companions, and finest courageous musicians I was ever going to meet. Together they were called 'The Monopoly'. Their singer had left them a week before. I knew he was good because I had seem him work. He was visually dynamic, and seemed to be able to play any instrument, and here was I who couldn't play anything, and had never sang in public before. I didn't think for one moment that they would play for me.

I still don't know to this day what made them say yes, and I don't suppose they would tell me, even if I asked. My feelings were a mixture of euphoria and apprehension. I felt lonely and somehow scared. When I was a small boy of nine I stole a basket weaving outfit from school. I told my mother I had won it for some reason or another. She believed me. I went to bed early that night and was allowed to have the light on to play with this award, as the school holidays started the following day. At my young age, I felt the cold room, and heard the sad movement of my thieving fingers as they rummaged through the box. The tall old-fashioned wardrobe looked awesome and black, and I cried to myself, not because I felt guilty - I cried because I felt lonely.

The next day I gave the ill-gotten gain to my younger cousin. I was highly praised by my mother and aunt for this unselfish action. I didn't own up to the crime - I hadn't the courage. I accepted the unearned gratitude freely. I haven't stolen since, but I remember the loneliness to this day.

Lonely and scared, yes, but I hadn't stolen this band. It was awarded to me by these players and I wasn't going to give it to anyone. I only hoped it could belong to me forever. Such a precious gift these people, and I began immediately to believe that I owned them. We all grew to love each other, and I'm sure they forgive me that foolish presumption.

Ray Froggatt, H Cain, Lou Clark and Len Ablethorpe were to achieve much in the next few years, but here we were on the very first day. H. Cain was a quiet introvert seventeen year old boy, with an infectious likeable attitude. His natural honesty was obvious, and his love for the guitar immense. His ability, though in its early stages demanded a great respect and his performance on this instrument has always been an extension of his personality. He always played with warmth, understanding and unselfishness; making his unique style an instant signature of a man who can really play. He was to become, and still is, a great strength to the future of our professional quest. He is a mechanic, a driver, an agent, a manager, an arranger, an adviser, a great guitar player, and the best friend you could hope to get in this sometimes so ugly world.

Len Ablethorpe was like colours. He stood out - six feet tall with bright red hair. He had a passion to be on a stage, and his dress sense could have been likened to a paranoid parrot, longing to be a peacock. His great loveable humour was the saviour of many a sad moment. In the early days though, he was a bit of a Mama's boy. He was only sixteen. He grew into one of the shrewdest toughest characters I've known, with an open, candid nature that was better for you than against you. He was the kind of drummer who knew what to play for all songs, never fancy - just solid, loud and in perfect time. A bass player's dream.

Lou Clark seemed to me to be rather posh. He was brought up by his lovely old aunt in Bridgnorth. His good education and well-spoken attitude I found very refreshing. He had 'A' levels in just about everything except 'washing'. He seldom changed his shorts or socks. He maintained he could never see the point. His musical talent for composing and arrangement, orchestration and conducting has very few equals, and his success reached world renown. This superb musician was our bass player.

With yours truly as the singer, this then was going to be our band. On Thursday of the week we formed I had to go and have the offending kidney removed. Slightly inconvenient but, ten days later we were rehearsing, stitches an' all - living proof of how cruel the unfair nickname 'The Slaughterhouse' to

Airport photo:
Frog; Mick; Len; H Cain

24

magnificent Dudley Road Hospital, and the kind skilful people who turn so much tragedy into joy. God bless you and ta!

We started working at the newly opened nightclub called 'Tito's'. Seven nights a week, we played four hours a night and we earned five pounds a week each. We never minded too much because we didn't think we were ready for the road yet. Nevertheless we all had the same wish to play at one of the bigger venues in our town; namely 'The Cedar Club' or the 'Elbow Room', where all the more established bands were doin' it. Bands like 'Denny Laine and the Diplomats', 'Carl Wayne and the Vikings', 'El Riot and the Rebels', 'Danny King and the Mayfair Set', 'Mike Sheridan and the Night Riders', Steve Gibbons and the Uglys'.

Our band was called 'Steve Newman and the Monopoly'. I was Steve Newman, a sort of cross between Paul Newman and Steve McQueen. Unfortunately when the young ladies saw a rather short-arse chap bop on the stage singing 'jump back baby, jump back, the magic which the names of those two illustrious gentlemen usually fires seemed to dim somewhat, almost instantaneously. Hence we thought it wise under the circumstances to change our name to 'Froggy and the Tadpoles'. Quite an endearing little monica, we thought. It also gave rise to much mirth among the younger element of our audience.

The band had informed me of the dangers of choosing the wrong name, by enlightening me to an occurrence at which they suffered considerable embarrassment. Having decided to call themselves 'The Buccaneers', in the hope that they might be thought upon as a devil may-care, swashbuckling outfit, an unfortunate promoter, in order to excite his full house and gain their attention, yelled 'where's The Buccaneers', only to be answered by scores of unenthusiastic drunken yobs with 'on the side of your buccin' 'ead'. Whereupon a slight fracas took place and the whole venue was smashed to bits. So I warn any youngsters planning this perilous road to give this matter more than just a little thought.

We did of course get our chance to play the better venues in our town, and we were becoming quite popular among the night club set. We were now beginning to enjoy playing and we were getting quite accomplished. We soon found out that this business is a great target-setter and inevitably we wanted to travel; new cities, universities, and the Continent, radio, TV. We needed an Agent. That was easier said than done. You see in those days small Agents had everything sewn up; small time charlies in every town pretending to be Lew Grade. When they got home from their milk-rounds they were phoning each other up, bragging about who they'd got on next week. Glorified promoters who

Beat Club T.V. Germany H Cain; Lou; Len; Frog

used to split commission with each other and bounce cheques on every band they could get hold of. They formed an association and called it 'AA', (the Agency Association). They had monthly meetings and blacklisted any band with whom they said they had had a problem. It didn't matter to them that some poor bastards had been stuck on the motorway all night, frozen and skint, trying to get to some prick or other's joke venue. Thank God these wankers have died out. They hadn't got the stamina or the love for the business to last for long.

I hated small Agents more than anything else. They seemed

useless to me and they always owed you money. Middlemen; leeches; feeding off young bands who were the lifeblood of the whole mess. Shame on them and good riddance.

It was out of the question to get signed up to a reputable London Agent. You had to have a recording Contract, and anyway we weren't ready for that scene yet.

Then one day a piece of luck came our way quite out of the blue. We were asked to play at The Belfry near Birmingham. Someone who was connected with the place had seen us

H Cain, Oxford Appollo

work at a club, and thought that we could be a good support for a bigger band. The Belfry was one of the biggest and most prestigious venues in the whole country. All the most famous bands played there. We were so excited about the whole thing that it became our everyday conversation for weeks. Nothing else mattered. We rehearsed every day and all day. Our music style changed often because we had to play other people's songs. We hadn't ventured bold enough to play any of our own yet, and at this time we were playing some Beach Boys' material. Our harmonies were a little odd but we'd got the rest of it right.

The big night came. We had all tarted up a bit - even Lou had a clean shirt on. Len looked like a stick of multi-coloured Blackpool rock. It was difficult to see what colour he wasn't wearing. We had a proper dressing room for the first time. Trouble was, we didn't have anything to change into! We played as good as we were able; at our best. The crowd liked us too, and we've never been very confident with dancing crowds, but these thought we were OK.

The two people who ran the Belfry gig were called John Parsons and John Sabel, and as luck would have it they were both Beach Boys fans. We were in! The Belfry became a regular gig for us, and because of this we began to get more confident. We started to expect applause and considered it quite natural to receive our well-earned appreciation. We were beginning to measure the applause from one song against another. Thus finding out which parts of our show needed changing. This unconscious progression gave rise to discussion amongst ourselves as to which direction our music should take. Our individual sounds were starting to interest us greatly. We were actually becoming aware of the need for better equipment. We began to discover our contemporaries and challenged their skill against ours.

Things were so difficult for us at the time, that this most beautiful period in our career was treated with matter of fact coolness and passed by almost unnoticed.

It's only when I take my thoughts back and mooch among the scattered litter of dead deeds, that I find and see again my friends growing; their young faces full of humour and hope, their hands and minds so eager to learn. I could see their natural talents shaping their time.

'O' gallant bird to break from your shell.
You wet and tired bedraggled creature.
Warm thyself in sunlight. Then soft, gold, and free are thee'

We do leap from year to year don't we? Landing here and there.

Carrying with us traces of silver thoughts from the people whose lives we touch. Enter tragedy! Should these memories bounce off me and pass?

John Parsons and John Sabel not only gave us invaluable experience through their kindness in booking us at their club, but they also became great friends. Their wonderful help and enthusiasm given so unselfishly, was to build us a foundation on which we would balance for several years. Indeed our first venture abroad to France was engineered by these two unforgettable people. Thrown into the deep end this dizzy band could hardly believe its luck. We were going to the Riviera - to Nice, the playground of the stars. Palm trees, mountains, blue sky and the Mediterranean sea. We didn't know what we were letting ourselves in for but we couldn't have cared less. What was there to question? We were to go to Paris first and work at the great Locomotive Club, then on to Nice for eight weeks' work in The Whiskey Club.

All of our live appearances at the Belfry had assured us that we were ready for anything.

Accommodation would be provided for us free of charge, but we had to provide our own travelling expenses to Paris. What a magnificent adventure this turned out to be. How snug those weeks sit in the small corner of my heart that I keep especially for France.

Chapter three

FRANCE

This fantastic business has an infuriating habit of giving you no time at all to prepare for anything. Indeed this opportunity came to us on a Monday, and by Thursday of the same week we were to arrive in Paris. Needless to say, we were broke, and our only transport was an old Ford Thames van, which had a very odd temperament indeed. Its radiator would boil dry at the very mention of a five mile journey, and a veritable orchestration of strange noises seemed to belch from every corner of its innermost being. The tyres would have been better employed on the side of a houseboat; its back doors had a most stubborn character, and the utmost discretion and tact had to be applied to the handle in order to get the slightest response as to the possibility that one might be favoured with an entrance to its rear capacity. The interesting knocking sound located somewhere beneath the floor in the axle area, had a most puzzling rhythm. Indeed, when accompanied by Len's sticks it formed a drum pattern quite unique to the realms of percussion. The battery, although very lively, had an almost suicidal nature. Several times a week it would dislodge itself from its cradle and have to be retrieved from under the wheels of some irate and white-faced motorist. The lights were aligned to suit plane spotting, and the indicators had severed all relations with the whole affair. The windscreen wiper had a peculiar circular motion that formed a quite pretty crescent, and gave one the impression that you were looking through a kaleidoscope. The overall look of this ailing creature gave one the image of what could only be described as a Victorian mousetrap. From a medical point of view, it's twilight years were, I'm sure, ever grateful and indebted to the inventor of string.

The first problem of our immediate expenses was solved by H. Cain's mother who, very daringly and generously, loaned us fifty pounds to cover the ferry fare, food and petrol to Paris. In those days fifty pounds was a substantial sum, and this lovely lady helped us without hesitation. Some people are so good, aren't they?

The second problem of the van was solved by a ten gallon drum of water, to be carried in the back in order to replenish loss from overheating. The rest we left in the hands of H. Cain and God.

This intrepid party of dreamers set off with a great passion in our hearts, and plenty of room in our heads for the realities we were about to experience.

Lou Clark had a great capacity to organise and so he was in charge of the booking arrangements for the ferry to Calais, also the budgeting of the expenses. He could speak French too, so we were doing okay up to now.

Halfway down the M1 stopping now and again to water the radiator, boat tickets in our pockets, rainbows in our eyes, guitars wrapped in blankets and music in our minds. Look out fame! Look out stars, moon, sky! Such energy all around us; deep with us, each other's hopes. Oh it's great to know you lads; it's great to be doing this. God knows where we were going but we were going together. This is our piece of life; we are living it. This journey together at this time can only be made by us. This will be our bit of history. History for us, to remain in our minds forever.

We boarded the ferry at 9.00 o'clock in the evening. The van had behaved superbly. Its exhaust barked a little as we entered the ferry car park, but it was a friendly bark, as if it were feeling cocky about having completed the first leg of the journey. As we left our four wheeled companion I'm sure I could detect a slight smile on the front of its grid; it could now cool and slumber in the ship's hold. We were due in Calais the next morning.

An uneventful night. We crashed out on the seats. Lou informed us that our budget wouldn't run to bunk charges. We were allowed a ferry breakfast, which we all ate with great gusto. Now we were ready for the day. The boat docked. All passengers were in their cars ready for the big exodus.

Our van started first time, and we were all set. The line of organised traffic moved like a great coloured caterpillar, its head disappearing into the cold dark morning. H. Cain mumbled a few well known profanities to himself and informed his well-breakfasted colleagues that the accelerator cable had snapped. The caterpillar seemed to break in half as the mobile section left us crippled. To push that van full of equipment off a ferry and up the 400 yard ramp, with a hundred tired impatient drivers behind, calling us names that at the very least disputed the validity of our parentage was no joke.

The accelerator cable on a Ford Thames van is more complicated than the space shuttle, and the useless suggestions by three very cold, fed up, grumpy musicians, was very little help to H. Cain, who was by this time underneath the van and covered with oil.

It was then that we met our first welcoming committee. Two huge French policemen armed to the teeth. As they gabbled on in a language that might just as well be Martian to me, I detected a tone that suggested a not-very-complimentary set of French endearments. Lou, thinking that silence was the better part of valour, decided not to understand them. After deducing in their budding Clouseau minds that we were English, they must have thought that we weren't worth bothering with, either to arrest or help! They wandered off muttering 'Anglaise merd', which I understand from Lou meant English shit!

I've often wondered what their comments were of this 'English shit' after the likes of my father who was a paratrooper during the Second World War, got his bollocks shot to bits helping to liberate them from a  tyrannical power that considered them to be less than shit. I suppose it's a case of human priorities living up to their usual shit standard.

With the ingenious use of a guitar string this enthusiastic guitar playing mechanic, H. Cain, got us mobile again with a repair that would have put any RAC or AA man to shame.

It was a beautiful day and France is such a lovely country, that we all felt God deserved a pat on the back for his kindness in showing us and allowing us to appreciate a small part of his wonderful work of art. England and France; the place we came from and the place we came to. The same colours splashed with Churchillian pride and confidence, fully honest and fair. The odd corruption of misused materials erected in error by some mortal architect who had dared to compete, failed to bespoil the maestro's original idea. Mere warts that will eventually fade and disappear, thus becoming once again, splashed colours.

This comical vehicle full of happy souls limping through the sometimes winding, sometimes open French roads, were heading for our first instructed destination; a small village about twenty miles from Paris. Here we were to telephone an Agent at his private house. He would then guide us verbally to his door. After two such calls we were still lost. We began to feel his impatience through the wires. After explaining to him where we had got to he decided to send one of his sons out on his moped to rescue us from our dilemma. He would be wearing a red anorak and standing beneath a large tree. All we had to do was carry on down the road until we saw him.

In these sort of situations it was quite common for the complete complement of heads to be all pushed forward side by side into the cab, eager-eyed, searching for this unknown saviour. Eventually a chorus of 'There 'e is!' echoed around our tin world. We were there. The boy was about fifteen. His friendly concerned smile and directional wave seemed like a welcome home. His thoughts upon the sight of this trampish dishevelled bunch of joy, was anybody's guess.

We had been travelling all day and the beautifully typically French stone housed we had arrived at looked like heaven. The red louvred roof tiles seemed to be rippling in the late afternoon sun. Small wrought iron balconies outside shutter-clad continental windows, willow trees and blossom smells talked and filled the air. A dog barked - not viciously but more chasing a stick in the parkish. Everything was sepia and rustic; quite lovely.

The old van rolled over the cobblestone yard and came to an uncertain halt. The engine gave an asthmatic wheeze, pre-ignitioned for a while, and then made a noise that could only be described as a 'wet fart', and then became silent. It was beginning to feel the journey, and it was in good company.

The Agent greeted us and introduced us to his extremely nice family. His wife, two sons and daughters seemed quite thrilled, for at that time to have an English band in your home was very unusual, not to say most fashionable too. I didn't like the Agent. He had a veneer of false friendship over him, a fat insincere face, pot-holed with two small watery eyes, which gave him a sinister look. His square mouth looked a perfect haven for lies. He informed us that, after a rest and dinner, he had an appointment for us in Paris. We had been booked into an hotel there and we would be spending three days there in order to perform the venues he had arranged for us. These performances were to ensure our expenses to enable us to continue to Nice for our eight week engagement at the famous Whisky Club. We were tired after travelling for almost three days, but, after a great French meal, a little rest and a few games of table football, natural youthful enthusiasm returned and we were looking forward to our first gig in Paris.

The Agent unwisely said that he would travel with us in the van and show us the way to the club and hotel. We said our goodbyes to the kind family and piled into the van. As H. Cain turned the key in the ignition the stunned vehicle gave a sharp squeak; a sort of rat-like discontented moan, before bursting into mechanical song. It soon realised that we were on our way again and accepted the fact by responding to the driver's request for reverse gear. An operation usually accompanied by the most horrendous metallic screeches, finally thumping with such violence as to occasion every head to hit the roof with such force that any semblance as to comfort in that area was quite unrecognisable, and the unfortunate interior roof life I'm afraid, was based beyond all medical assistance.

We arrived in Paris at about 9.30 pm. The lights of this magnificent city set of triggers of excitement through us all. The nightclub had a rather seedy appearance. A flashing half-lit neon light about a steel sheeted black painted one-time window seemed to conjure up a picture of a city's sigh. It occupied an area that could have been the flaking skin of Paris. The old Paris peeling away and hanging like chrysalis remains to the very edge of this beautiful new butterfly.

In spite of its appearance and locality the club had a raw, energetic appearance. We weren't disappointed. After all we hadn't been used to anything better, and anyway we couldn't wait to play again, so in we went.

Inside it was just like any other club we had been to. No fancy flashing disco lights (they hadn't been invented yet!), a big stage - all clubs had big stages. The emphasis was on live music in those days. All the kids wanted to see a Band. Nowadays we make the records to put the DJs in work and in return they criticise our work, then call their pick of our work, their show. Then they charge money to play our work to people who buy our work in places where we used to work, and so put us out of work! Funny how it works isn't it?

We were surprised to find about eight other bands in the place; all of them French. Lou, having heard some of their conversations told us that it was a contest of some sort with hundreds of francs for the winners. We thought it was time to surround the Agent to find out was going on. He admitted that it was a contest, but he had entered us to get our expenses to Nice. 'What if we don't win?' we protested. 'You already have' he replied. We felt cheated having to cheat, but we hadn't any choice. The unsuspecting French bands launched into the contest with great spirit, with their own loyal supporters voicing their enthusiastic approval. They all did great. Then came our turn. We were introduced to almost complete silence, and every song received the same non-commitment from the crowd. We walked off to the sound of our own boots. When it was announced that we had won, all hell broke loose. They had cottoned on to the fraud. We were ushered out whilst the arguing was going on and so escaped what could have been quite a difficult moment. On the way to the hotel the Agent apologised for any embarrassment we may have felt and gave us 100 francs out of the spoils to tide us over until the next day. We arrived at the hotel. The Agent would see us checked in and call us the next day.

What a dump this hotel turned out to be. The whole building was extremely narrow and very tall. As we walked in the thick brown half-glazed door a most nauseating smell hit us straight between the eyes. I can only describe it as been a cross between the gusset of a postwoman's drawers and sheep dip! The dank far corner housed a filthy excuse for a reception counter littered with useless brass items. Unfriendly squares of thick brown glass formed a canopy above the head of the most sinister woman I have ever seen. Her nose had three different dimensions, as if it had been modelled by a potter with arthritis. The hair on her face gave her large toothless mouth the appearance of a tear in a Harris Tweed coat, and her chin, like a skin covered swing boat moving grotesquely as she uttered her only English word, 'Passports'. 'Passports'; in exchange for which she gave us one key between us.

Our room on the top floor defies description but it would have made a first class kiln for smoking herrings.

The whole thing was becoming great fun. The lovely humour of my fantastic young friends was beginning to show. This was going to be a great trip. We tossed a coin to see who would sleep in the van to guard the equipment. Len lost. 'Goodnight Len, see you tomorrow'. 'Goodnight lads, you bastards'. We talked in the dark for a while about the Agent. Could we trust him? We didn't know, but it was too late now anyway. We wondered how everyone at home was. What was Nice going to be like. 'Wonder how Len is getting on in the van?' '**** 'im'. 'Yea'. 'Goodnight'. 'See you tomorrow'.

It was the next day. The sun was out. We didn't have to work until 6.00 o'clock. We had a hundred francs to spend and we were in Paris. We all had a wash except Lou, and we went sightseeing. All those famous places; the Opera House, the Tower, the Arc de Triomphe, Madame Tussaud's, the River Seine, the Paris bridges, the Metro, Notre Dame. We saw them all in a day. Postcards were sent home to those we loved. We even sent them to people we knew who didn't like us, just to knock them sick. What a day! Full of noise, laughter and fun. Our gig on that night was at the Locomotive Club - a better venue altogether, and the people loved us. We played for three hours non stop. We were paid the rest of our expenses by the Agent and he wished us luck. I'll see you boys in eight weeks, at the same hotel'.

It was H. Cain's turn to sleep in the van and we decided to get an early start in the morning. Lou had mapped our route out after pricing the toll payments on the motorways and he thought it would be financially more viable to go over the Alps. We set off at 3.00 am; our first stop should be Lyon. We zipped through the dark French night at a fair, untroubled lick. The van seemed to like the cool night movement. There were times when it sounded almost saloon-like!

The sky was just on the turn when we arrived at Lyon. A drinks trailer was open in the main square so we stopped for coffee and a sandwich. Lou asked the gentleman behind the counter the direction to the road across the Alps. He looked at our vehicle, and then at us, adopted the frown of a puzzled giraffe, shook his head, and said nothing. The coffee was welcome and warming and we were beginning to feel comfortable in this strange country.

We were keen to move on. There was along way ahead of us and our spirits were high. The sun came early that morning and we had been driving for six hours before we reached the foot of the Alps. The road opened out into a high waste land. We could see wire fencing and armed guards with dogs. There were earth movers and yellow diggers scattered here and there, silent and menacing. The strange dead trees leaning obscenely from the rocky slopes, looked fit only to crack and fall to the black ugly earth. Our noisy, rattling, backfiring arrival on to the scene caused dog ears to stand and turn forward. The same puzzled look from beneath peaked police caps was becoming commonplace. This sad, dreary guarded scene could only be evidence that man was digging here.

Here we began our ascent on to the mountain road to the Alps. As Hannibal had many years before, but at least he had elephants. All we had was a clapped out Ford Thames van.

The road that was to be our assault track onto the Alps was as steep as you can imagine. First gear, and five miles an hour were all our old faithful van could manage. With three or four water refills we made the top of the climb. We were on the Alps. Next stop - the South of France.

Well, what can one say about the beauty? These fairy-tale mountains simply burn into the very centre of your existence. The higher we climbed the more powerful the feeling of invisibility. We were a tiny nonsense moving the hot red dust from road to verge, as we moved gently but confidently on. As we climbed higher and deeper into our journey we could see snow above us and white, sun scorched rock formations below. Sometimes they looked like huge cavities in a giant's tooth. There wasn't time for us to stop and sightsee. We had to be in Nice the following morning. On and on we ventured, occasionally refilling the radiator, then filling the petrol tank from our supplies in the spare can we carried. The road, for most of the time, had a sheer drop of hundreds of feet to the one side, requiring the driver's concentration to be one hundred percent. Apart from one worrying moment H. Cain's performance was magnificent. A huge green flying creature entered one of the windows and landed on his lap. Now H. Cain, not being overly fond of the insect life form on this planet, gave a strangled shriek and promptly left the vehicle! We were doing approximately 30 mph at the time, and massive panic broke out among the remaining souls on board, as flailing arms desperately made lunatic lunges for the wheel. Between us we managed to bring the startled van to a halt and our uninvited green invader left, quite unperturbed.

After our hysterical laughter had passed we continued with all our windows firmly shut.

Darkness began to fall and we were still in the mountains, but we were making good progress. By this time, after some sixteen hours of driving, H. Cain complained of feeling rather tired. It was my turn to take the wheel.

We ate paloni sausage and bread, drank water, and continued. Around seven hours later, still on the Alps in pitch darkness, there was an almighty bang, followed by a horrifying crunch from somewhere beneath the van. I stopped and looked round at my wide eyed newly awakened comrades. 'What the **** was that?' were Len's first words for eight hours. H. Cain, as always, was the first out with the torch while we all sat mortified, waiting for the verdict. We could hear thumping and grinding noises that sounded like cracking, tearing metal, giving way to H. Cain's physical onslaught against the offending problem. A final r r r i i p p and clatter suggested he had thrown something over the cliff edge. He returned to us, exclaiming that everything was all right now. Apparently the loud bang was a spring snapping in half, and the crunching was the exhaust pipe and silencer hitting the road, causing it to mangle up, rendering it useless. The frenzied amputation of this system was followed by its disposal over the side of the Alps. We looked at each other with some dismay when he told us to continue, as he returned to his rudely awakened slumber.

I started the van, feeling somewhat hesitant. The stricken vehicle belched out a roar similar to a dozen concrete mixers all starting up together. Our old friend moved off smoothly, if not a little noisily, causing I'm sure all wild life in a radius of three miles to be convinced that it was time to go to ground.

Our descent from the Alps began as the sun broke through, and daylight unveiled a sort of tropical scene. The roadside plants were different and the rocks and sky had a sort of Greek appearance. We were nearly there. Everyone in the van woke up as the light came and H. Cain suggested that he take over the driving again. I was tired but not sleepy. Excitement began to enter us all again.

As we neared sea level, people, and other cars came into view. We had become very used to the noise of our van but every head turned as we clanked, rumbled and clattered by. A motorcycle cop followed us for about five miles before pulling alongside. We all smiled and waved to him. His response was negative as he sped away, probably thinking 'Anglaise merd'. It's just as well he didn't stop us because we didn't have any work permits or green card insurance. Our situation at that time couldn't include bureaucratic luxuries. 'NICE 5 kms'; the sign was a sight for sore eyes. We arrived right on the sea front. I remember Len referred to it as 'the Prom'. Good old Len! First we found the club. It was 11.00 am. It had taken us twenty hours to get from Paris. Now we could have twelve hours' rest before we were due to play.

The Whisky Club was again typical; dark decor, mirrored walls, a small dance floor in front of a stage, which was the full width of the room. The bar occupied the corner area at the opposite end. It was a groundfloor place and held about three hundred people when full. An hour after our arrival we were all set up on stage and ready for our performance. A band in those days didn't feel the need for masses of equipment. Ours for instance consisted of two VOX AC 30 amps, one Selmar Bass Rig, a kit of Ajax drums, a small 100 watt pa system, two vocal mikes, plus the stands and a case for all our leads.

The owner of the club, a man named Max, gave us the address of our accommodation, a large room in an old building which contained four beds and a shower, very clean and all we needed. It was within walking distance from the club so we found an eight week resting place for our gallant, four wheeled hero.

As we sat around a table in Le Georges Cafe drinking coffee, we planned our strategy for the eight weeks' stay in Nice. One meal a day would have to be our food intake, the first fifty pounds would have to be put aside for the repayment of the loan from H. Cain's mom. Petrol money home had to be saved. We might also need to buy some parts for the van in order to tackle the journey home. In short, the order of the day was to be careful handling of all earnings and Lou was to be in charge. Such an important board meeting has never been held at any level of business.

Playing times for the duration of our stay were as follows: six hours per night (to be played in 3/4 hour stints) with fifteen minutes break between each stint, Monday till Saturday. On Sunday an afternoon performance of four hours plus the usual six hours on the same night. You may think, as we did, that this was quite a mammoth task, but this experience proved to be a most valuable lesson in all the skills and stage presentation that an entertainer and musicians could need.

The vast amount of material needed to accomplish this commitment compelled us to include some of our own songs ... the beginning of an operation that in later years provided world hits. There was a steady stream of holiday-makers among our audiences, but we had the local regular kids who came along most nights, some becoming very good friends and loyal fans. Our discipline never faltered as the weeks passed. We honoured the rulings of our first day meeting, curbing our natural youthful longings to spend and have fun.

As I recall the teachings of these early days I am deeply convinced of the unnecessary pain that we, the artistes, inflict upon ourselves simply by making ourselves believe that we are in competition against the business.

You see, I firmly believe that popular music is purely a matter of personal taste among the same public whom we all try to reach. It is certainly true that the organisations that run our industry, for example the publishers and the recording companies) are compiled of human beings who, in themselves, are members of the public and it is folly to believe that these people would deliberately frustrate you by not making your work available to the popular music market.

Although they are not always right, they must be considered to be also entertained by your offering in order to market your work with any conviction. Their opinion of the climate must be accepted for the sake of the business. In short, one company will turn you down but another will accept you. Personal taste, you see, not competition.

In some cases, your audience will find you before the business will, making live performance vital in order to remember the reason for your being involved, which is primarily to entertain people and to learn

your trade. Make no mistake, you will always be learning, because people's personal tastes are changing constantly. I have learned that the frustrations are not manufactured by the business. They are simply life's frustrations suffered by everyone. The trouble is, raw material for our trade cannot be grown and you can't dig it from the earth. It must come from your heart and mind, thus making it doubly hard to accept the criticism of your artistic creation.

It's like someone telling you that your child is ugly, you must remember that with whatever handicap or unfortunate deficiency a child is born with, in most cases it is perfect to its mother; so you must never forget your own personal love for your song.

When a recording company or publisher decides to release an artiste's work, all the cogs must turn in their favour. Their product must be accepted by the media. They have to hope and work hard for radio plays. Retailers have to consider their product worthy to stock, without sale or return. They sweat for favourable reviews. Distribution has to be on the ball. You see, they too have their critics and their 'child' is their good name and their money.

We the artists are not here to be judged by our peers, the degrees of our skills are irrelevant to each other. Our appeal to the public can be many things. In some cases sexual attraction can do the trick. In others, overall sound and feel, dress fashion takes part. Youthful energy, married to loud noise, stage charisma, romantic interpretation. All types of music played and sung sometimes adequately and sometimes with sheer genius. The truth is, we are all in the same game, and however accomplished we play, if we connect then we are doing it right. Surely we are all good in our own way.

> There is a great talent within you,
> and if you use it,
> it will shine like the sea.
> And if you do not use it,
> it will run from you.
> And if within its use,
> you touch one person's heart.
> Then you will have touched the sun.

When you look at these thoughts, which were to grow and make more sense within me as I gained more experience you can see the importance of having the right people around you when you're in the process of creating music and chasing dreams.

I had the perfect combination of true friendship and music-making chemistry in these three young and eager to learn musicians.

It is impossible to measure my feelings of gratitude for the unselfish understanding, confidence and music knowledge they gave me. To play my songs with such love and care. To show their need of me so beautifully and accept my need of them so gracefully. What more is there to receive for a man to become a man.

The eight weeks soon passed and we had been very successful in our endeavours. An appearance on a national French television programme in Monaco gave us our first taste of public broadcasting. We loved it! There was only one worrying moment for us, it was when Len went missing and we were due to go on stage. We separated to look for him. H. Cain eventually found him in a cafe. He had been there for two hours, with empty pockets and a cup of coffee to pay for. He hadn't realised that he hadn't any money with him so he pretended to make the coffee last. Here was this French cafe owner, slowly drying cups, looking furtively across at an English youth, six feet tall with bright red shoulder length hair, dressed in all colours of the rainbow, looking like a demented clown who had been sprayed by a painter with shell-shock. Five francs rescued him and all was well.

The time came to leave Nice and make our way back home. First to Paris to collect our boat tickets from the Agent, and then our triumphant return to Blighty. We informed Max, the club owner, of our arrangements with the Agent, which produced an uncertain frowning look. He warned us that things might not go as we had planned and gave us a sealed letter with a Paris address, a sort of 'life-line' he called it.

Our return to our well rested van found it looking very quiet and rather ill. The offside rear end had completely collapsed onto the wheel as a result of the damaged spring. Now, to get a spring for a Ford Thames van on the French Riviera is like trying to get a pair of Y fronts to fit Cyril Smith; so it was once again left to the ingenuity of H. Cain.

After careful inspection H. Cain's damage report was as follows, 'The exhaust is a write-off so we will have to put up with the noise; but we can't move with the spring in this state!' The van spring was made up of four strips of steel, two inches wide, and sandwiched together in a bow shape. These had separated at each end and become flat. H. Cain jacked the unfortunate vehicle up in order for the spring to form its natural bow shape. He then took six guitar capos (which are small clamps used to hold down the strings of the instrument) and placed one on each end of each leaf of the spring, thus allowing the component to retain its shape and strength after the removal of the jack. Absolute genius!! We were on our way home.

Yan Xavier, a local boy, was going to Paris and he knew the flat road, avoiding the mountains. He would show us the way in return for a lift there. He'd got himself a deal.

We wanted to make the journey non-stop so, while we loaded the van, H. Cain volunteered to get some food so that we wouldn't need to eat expensive cafe food on the way. Not being able to read French though, he returned with three packs of dog biscuits and two chocolate eclair making outfits! Ho! Hum!

Before finally leaving we all decided to send our final postcards home. Lou Clark would sometimes despair at our lack of education, by his standards, and I recall at this time a small exchange between him and Len as to how one spent 'auntie'. Lou informed the puzzled enquiring drummer that there was no such word as 'auntie' and that it was an endearing term by which very young children were encouraged to call their aunt. The disgruntled Len remained adamant that there must be such a spelling, as he had always called his aunt 'Auntie Gin'. 'Even if there was such a word', retorted the impatient Lou, 'You shouldn't be using it at the age of eighteen'. Lovely memories.

Our return to Paris was smooth and trouble free. We were happy to be going home and held a proud contentment for what we had achieved. After so many hours of entertaining under our belts we were wealthy in artform. We had to be one of the best non-recording bands around.

As we had half expected, our meeting with the Agent did not materialise and so we were without boat tickets. You get let down a lot in this darker side of the business and this was our first taste of trickery. Max's letter came immediately into use. Not knowing what to expect we rang the bell of a large, very posh looking house in the centre of Paris. The brass sign told Lou that it was a medical clinic of some kind. An elderly lady with a very high cheekboned face, making her look extremely French, answered our call; she smiled, took the letter and politely, in English, asked us to wait in a reception room. Fifteen minutes later she returned with an elderly gentleman who informed us that they would take a sample of blood from each of us. If we were well and willing, a pint from each of us would raise the boat fare home. One thing about our band was that we were game for anything! The whole thing was over in an hour. The process, performed in what looked like very professional surroundings, was painless and rewarding. There is possibly a French policeman walking around now quite happily, with a pint of English merd blood in him.

The next stop was Dunkirk; we had missed the boat from Calais. This was the first time that we ran head on with a French Official. Our arrival on the quayside caused every Customs Officer to almost jump out of his skin and the van, by this time, sounded like seven Russian tanks. Occasions like this call for the old Brummie ploy of acting dead thick. We were asked to leave the vehicle and go to the office. Three Customs men approached our hissing, steam blowing friend with the utmost caution. Their pained expressions and shaking heads suggested a confusion that must have been felt by the first Australian deportee on seeing his first kangaroo and thinking it was a big rabbit. The request for our passports, green card insurance, work permits and equipment carnet, was followed by us just handing over our passports and telling them that we didn't think we had to have anything else. The irate Customs Officer almost had a seizure! His blood pressure shot up to danger level and his broken English sounded positively lunatic. The office was full of law abiding British tourists, all of whom took a dim view of these young layabouts who were letting the side down.

Our passports were thrown at us and we were told to leave France immediately. The whole place was silent and every passenger, crew and

Customs Officer, watched us enter the van. As H. Cain started it up there was an almighty roar, followed by an ear-splitting backfire, as everyone stared wide eyed. When we moved forward up the ramp of the boat we could no longer hold our mirth. The band just fell into fits of belly laughter, whilst everyone on the deck stood poker-faced. What an exit!

Goodbye France. You were great!

It isn't yours, put it back Brownie!!!

$\mathcal{C}$*hapter* *four*

POLYDOR RECORDS

The white cliffs of Dover hit our eyes, as they had the eyes of millions of people before us. Homeward weary travellers, victorious and defeated soldiers; invaders; smugglers; the luckless, landless, lonely desperate villains, and royal personage, some living and some long forgotten. You can almost hear their spent lives, their hopes, tears and dreams blowing across the wind. One day our echoes will follow them, but for the moment we were going home.

The ageing, worn out, travel-soiled vehicle coughed, barked, clattered and roared through the Customs area, looking magnificent in its sad ruin, attracting its usual vast audience. It gave a sort of middle-of-the-road performance, great comedy laced with moments of true pathos, with vocal power that would have put the great Caruso to shame. Its 'liable to do anything' ad lib quality kept every eye glued to its riveting presence. A marvellous professional. I've often thought that if we could have commanded half as much attention we would have had a hit record years ago.

The last leg of our homeward journey was a 'piece of cake'. Arriving back in Birmingham with a tale to tell. We had taken Len home first. He lived in the living quarters of the Memorial Hall at Henley-in-Arden, where his parents were the caretakers. Rose and Joe Ablethorpe and Len's brother Terry became, and still are, a second family to me. Terry was also a drummer in a band that followed more avant-garde blues tradition. His admiration for our band gave us enormous pleasure as we looked to his band with such pupilistic awe. Len's family were a noisy, joyful clan, who seemed to revel in each others presence. There was a powerful parent/children bond which created interest in each other. Happy vibrations coupled with normal family crisis gave rise to beautiful comedy and love. Their lives had been hard and poor; but their wealth in attitude and honesty was obvious and true.

Lou was the next to be taken home. He lived in lodgings with a family called 'the Browns'. They lived in a flat above a dentist's surgery in Aston. I'm sure they will forgive me for saying that through no fault of their own, their accommodation had a dingy and lost appearance; but Ma Brown, her daughter Pam, son Peter and the sinister Uncle Bill, shared all they had with Lou. Ma Brown was a quiet woman who chain-smoked. Pam was a very cute teenage girl who found it necessary to flirt as many teenage girls do, with every boy who came through the door. Young Peter was a typical cheeky kid who grew up to become quite an accomplished guitar player in his own right, and Uncle Bill never uttered anything beyond a grunt to anyone. In this environment Lou seemed to me to be very out of place and lonely.

His home in Bridgnorth was a complete contrast. It was a house where you would imagine one of Enid Blyton's Famous Five to live. A spotless, orderly home with his lovely old aunt in charge. A huge ginger tom slept all day in a box by the large cast iron open fire. A massive grandfather clock stood majestically on the first turn of the stairs. On the occasions of my visits there, tea would be laid out on the large table beneath the window. A pure white linen table-cloth would be decorated with diamond cut, jam covered bread slices, rock cakes and milk. A photograph of the nine year old school blazered Lou stood on the window-ledge. Conversations of the church choir and Uncle Batt's vegetable garden were the norm. Lou's sister worked at the hospital and his elder brother had emigrated to Germany.

I don't know why, but the change, because of time and the natural growth of things, provokes tears within me. All things are turning. The sounds of children we know, pass, to become the ordinary sounds of the world.

There are those who are born and then die without ever seeing a blade of grass. There are the hungry who cling to the breast of mankind only to find it dry and empty. There are the killers who slash at the innocent, there are the greedy who scoff at the poverty in others. There are the thieves who rob only themselves. There are the houses in Bridgnorth that will become empty and then full again. Lou Clark's ambition, commonsense and drive were going to take him far away from his early life; and his first move was to Ma Browns to nurture his great talent within our band.

H. Cain's son Jon contemplates in the garden in Jersey.

H. Cain then took me home to a house in Kingstanding where I lived with my four brothers, my sister and her husband, and my mother. I have to explain here why I left home shortly after this period. We have always been a close family and our mother's example taught us to value each other without sugary, false sentiment. She was made a widow through the Second World War. A young girl of twenty-three years of age, with three children to raise; my brother Jim, my sister Jean and me. She had very little help from anyone but she never failed us. She had to live in lodgings with us and worked hard in factories to feed us and clothe us. There surely have been times when her life must have seemed hopeless and cruel; but she kept her time to love us.

There must have been so much love, because I feel so much of it now. She eventually married again, and we became a full family once more with four more brothers to enrich our lives even further. The first of these brothers to arrive sadly died in his cot at the age of six months; but our mother still remembered his birthday every year, quietly and privately. He is still referred to as 'our John'. This incredible lady has always shared her love and affection equally amongst us; no favourites. We were all the same, and none received more than the other. She has always been frank and outspoken, also warm and understanding. A great fighting machine when we were threatened, and a great strength when frightened. She was always poor, but we were always loved. To disappoint her would be unthinkable. Our manners were of paramount importance. The words 'please' and 'thank you' essential. So here was I, a young man with a desire to reach out and create music. I felt a need to live among other people, to put myself in uncertainty. It was the area I had to leave. I wanted to be daring and unconventional. I wanted to feel brave and independent.

I didn't realise then that I needed people more than anyone I know.

H. Cain finally brought the van to its final destination, his home in Mansfield Road, Aston. He lived in a terraced house that was situated at the rear of some other terraced houses. There was a long, narrow entry paved with blue bricks which made the heels of your boots sound like

Frog's brother Ken and sister-in-law Joan.
Jersey is so nice this time of year.

ricocheting bullets. It was a house without a bathroom. I suppose pre-war architects felt that working people didn't need to bathe, but at least they won't ever have to bathe their souls like some of the bastards who designed those hovels. The house was damp and dark. As a result of this both his parents suffered from bronchitis, a legacy from forty years of Councils who probably never gave a thought to the thousands of people they had condemned to this way of life. H. Cain lived here with his mother and father. The three of them seemed to have the same sort of personality. They were all quiet, but very friendly. His father was a musician in an old accordion band. He had a lovely calm manner about him, and he could make anything from guitar parts to clothes driers. There was a little of the mad inventor in him. His shed, in the small garden, was the most interesting place in the world. He seemed to have every odd thingumajig you could lay a name to. He was kind and clever. His head was full of ideas and his hands were always busy in work.

His mother on the other hand had an endearing scattiness about her. Her imagination would run wild with her at times. I remember when Ronald Biggs escaped; she swore she had seen him walking down Mansfield Road with a mac and dark glasses on! She spoke slowly and quietly but it was obvious that she was nobody's fool. She had, and still has, a smashing sense of humour and I love her very much.

Well, we were all home, our adventure was over but we still had many more to come. Nothing in the future could scare us. We were ready to play anywhere and we felt that we could hold our own against anyone. Our band was confident. We were writing our own songs so we began to really want to make a record. It was going to be sooner than we thought possible.

At this time the music industry was undergoing considerable changes. The existing bands in Birmingham realised that their approach had to be more sensational if they were going to follow in the footsteps of the Spencer Davis Group and the Moody Blues, both of whom by this time had achieved world acclaim for their great music. The former because of the multi-talented Steve Winwood and the latter because of the idea to form a band from what they considered to be the best players from 1all the local bands in town. This idea was tried again. Carl Wayne, Ace Kelford and Bev Bevan from The Vikings teamed up with Roy Wood from The Nightriders and Trevor Burton from the Mayfair Set. These exceptional musicians became a band, who in my opinion, were the most original, exciting rock band of their time. The idea of smashing television sets and cars on stage amid floods of stunning lights, whilst playing fantastic Roy Wood songs, was to take the world by storm. Their dress and antics brought about the beginnings of visual theatricals twinned with musical excitement, so often used right up to this day. From then on a band's performance became a show performance. Smoke bombs and all kinds of gimmickry started to be used, and still is used, by all manner of heavy metal bands. I am firmly convinced that this thunderous, magnificent entertainment is an extension of the fortunate birth of a band which became known to the world as 'The Move'.

I don't know if it is the same in other cities, but in Birmingham amongst the band fraternity a great feeling of admiration is felt when one of the local bands make it into the big time. I can remember all of us gathering at the Cedar Club to watch The Move perform at a time when their first record had hit the charts. I felt a great inspiration to work harder and try to emulate their success.

Our band, like many others at that time, decided to include some theatricals into our show. After considering many ideas we settled on the spectacle of a public hanging during our performance. I wrote a song called 'The Hangman'. The idea was for me to be led off to the gallows whilst the band played frantic music amid flashing lights. My hands would be tied behind my back; I would then be put on to the scaffold, the trapdoor would be released, I would drop with the rope around my neck and bite a blood capsule. The lights would be blacked out, I would make my way back to the band in the dark and when the lights were put on I would be standing with the band to finish the song. Sounds simple doesn't it?

Firstly, we needed the gallows. It would have to be big and impressive. Also it would have to be designed so that it could be built and dismantled very quickly.

H. Cain and myself began to design and construct our new idea. First we bought ten pounds worth of timber and sixty five-inch bolts. We built a set of gallows that would have struck fear into the heart of the most cold-blooded killer in history. Now we had to find a way to ensure that I would not be actually killed! We decided that if we constructed a platform beneath the gallows the exact height between the end of the rope and my feet, this would break my fall. Then I would be able to take the strain manually, and so complete the illusion of an actual hanging. With me spitting the blood from the capsule it should look quite convincing. Now we were ready to try it out. It worked at our rehearsal and we were ready to try it out in public.

The Mackadown public house was, as usual, packed to the seams.

The huge concert room buzzing with the sounds of happy Saturday night people, some talking about the Aston Villa performance and some, Birmingham City and its usual fight for survival in the First Division. There was also the odd comment about the strange sight of the massive gallows situated at the side of the stage.

We had been well received by the crowd and the time came for the hanging song. The frantic music began and I was led off the stage by our roadie, Phil O'Brien, who had donned a black hood and cloak. I climbed the wooden steps onto the gallows. The rope was placed around my neck and every eye in the house was trained on this peculiar sight. The trapdoor was sprung and I dropped onto the hidden platform. Unfortunately the noose slipped from my neck. As I lunged in full flight to correct it my movement caused me to hit the platform wrongly. The result of this gave rise to a trampoline effect, ejecting me from the contraption and flinging me forward with such force that I wiped out three tables full of drinks and knocked about twenty people into a huge writhing heap. The shouts and screams of panic stricken women, with threats of unimpressed drunken men, occasioned a hasty retreat to the stage where the band, although in fits of laughter were still playing the music. I gazed with disbelief from the stage at the incredible carnage I had left in my wake. The whole scene was getting uglier as the innocent spectators were recovering. We finished the song and wished a rapid goodnight before things got worse and out of hand. As we were rushing from the stage a girl handed me her hanky, informing me that I had cut my lip. At least the blood capsule had looked realistic but I had quite forgotten about it. We left the building, the Manager, some very angry people and the equipment to our very gallant roadie, Phil. He told us later that our fee was split up between the bewildered customers.

We had another go at the hanging later on and at that time Phil O'Brien forgot to erect the safety platform, resulting in me being actually hung. I was told later that it took thirty minutes to revive me, and I had a rope burn around my neck for six months.

From then on we decided to leave the theatricals out of our

performance as we didn't seem very efficient in that area. Anyway, Len pointed out that it would be very inconvenient to have to find another singer at this stage. He could be so wise at times.

A month or two passed and we were now one of the most sought after bands in our local area. In retrospect I suppose the interest was because we were so different. We didn't perform any Top Twenty songs, which is what most bands did, so I believe that people found our original material, mixed with lesser known songs, very refreshing.

We never have been an outfit that people found easy to dance to, but our music policy has always leaned towards the careful choice of lyric content, and at that time people were beginning to show great lyric awareness in their musical pursuits.

We were settling into a style that needed an audience of minds rather than movement. As always this business, in its usual inconsistent manner, was leaping and shouting opportunity at everyone in it from all angles. The way of it seemed to me to be very confusing, so we grabbed everything that looked remotely like a chance to move forward.

John Parsons came to us one day with great news. Polydor Records had moved into London from Europe. They had opened an office in Oxford Street and this vast company were sponsoring new agencies in all major cities in Great Britain. Their aim was a connection with the Adsel Agency in Birmingham. This Company was one of the agencies that Polydor had decided to be involved with. The Agency was headed by Arthur Smith, who at that time, was the Manager of the Applejacks, a Birmingham band who were riding high with a hit record called 'Tell Me When'. We were recommended to Arthur Smith by John Parsons and a record test was arranged for us at a local studio called Hollick and Taylor. We were told that top recording people would be there from Polydor Records, London to judge our recording potential. This was a marvellous break for us and we were told to prepare three songs. We decided not to panic and change our style to a more conventional type of song. We stuck to our material plus a song by a little known artiste called Bob Dylan. None of us had been into a recording studio before and, unlike today, there was little or nothing in the trade papers to inform you what they were like, so it was quite a frightening prospect for us and at the back of our minds was the dread of failing.

The day of our test was eased by the kindness and help of John Taylor, who owned the studio. Sensing our distress, he did everything possible to make us feel like professionals. We have never forgotten him for that. A few modern-day engineers could learn a great deal from him.

The Polydor men arrived and we were introduced. They were Johnny Hawkins and Richard Hill. Later these two men were to write a smash hit musical called 'The Canterbury Tales' but today they were our judges.

Having been told to begin we found it puzzling that we were told to stop several times throughout the first song. We quite naturally thought that we were doing something wrong. Our comments to each other, which must have been heard in the control room were obviously causing some hilarity and we were put at ease by a voice telling us that they had almost got the sound to each instrument right, and they were ready to start recording. They they thanked us for our patience. How kind.

Our three songs were now recorded. Johnny Hawkins, Richard Hill, Arthur Smith and John Taylor came through the control room door. 'Well done lads'. I think it was Richard Hill speaking. 'Our policy is to let the artistes know within a week of our decisions.' My heart sank. I was convinced they didn't like us '... but in this case' he continued, 'we are pleased to tell you that from now on you are Polydor recording artistes'. I was so proud of us. We had a recording contract. I saw the eyes and faces of my friends full of disbelief and joy. We were young, and so happy. I felt a great love for them inside of me and I wondered at this moment as we seemed to skip in time with all things. 'You may think that this is the end of your troubles' one of them had broke my thoughts, 'but they are just beginning, anyway, Good Luck'. We never knew how right he was.

IN the current welter of progressive sounds and pop experimentation one thing is getting lost—melody. As more and more guitarists' fingers fly ever faster over the fretboards and more musicians attempt to break free of formal restrictions, it becomes really refreshing to hear a catchy song with a pleasant accompaniment.

Just as American country music is scoring in this way, so is Raymond Froggatt, as you will find out by listening to his Polydor album *The Voice And Writing Of Raymond Froggatt* or his latest single *Movin' Down South*. But Raymond is experimenting in his way too—with a full orchestra.

The Froggatt group started off in Birmingham about three years ago, later moving down to London where they played places like the Speakeasy and the usual run of folk clubs. Raymond enjoyed this period but felt that it wasn't leading anywhere. "It was a dead end," he told me. "We were playing electric folk and so were a lot of other people as well. We decided to get out and create something of our own."

Orchestra

And this they have achieved. "We recorded with an orchestra and it went O.K., although we had a big start with our knowledge of arranging and orchestration," explained Raymond. "We tried a concert in February with the Midland Light Orchestra at the Belfry in Birmingham and that was a big success."

Since then Raymond has repeated the performance at Ronnie Scott's Club in London, and has another gig with a 50-piece orchestra lined up for Birmingham in October. He hopes to do more shows of this sort, and it's an expensive business, but he believes that this sort of show can help break down the barriers between classical music and pop—from both sides.

He has found working with middle-aged professional musicians used to playing

FROGGATT BRINGS BACK MELODY– BUT WITH STRINGS

classical music an exciting experience, and the musicians have enjoyed it as well. "A lot of compromise is needed when you get a bunch of long-hairs amongst the middle aged," he said. "It takes a lot of time and effort to get over complications with volume and different attitudes to music, but they play what they read in front of them. At Scott's they really got going when they felt the atmosphere; they even began to sweat!

"In London these musicians are used to playing with pop people and they know what to expect but it was more difficult in Birmingham with the Midland Light Orchestra. It was strange to see a middle aged woman playing her violin with her handbag at her side, but even these ladies got the audience reacting. They start smiling because they can't believe the

reaction when they are used to the very formal concert atmosphere."

You might think that such musicians would play very competently but without much feeling, but that's not so. "We have to try and inject the excitement we feel," says Raymond. "If you want them to play with a lot of attack, they will do it. With the Midland, we just went through things once, and they had got it straight away."

The orchestration is worked out by Raymond's bass player Louis Clark, who took music at G.C.E. A-level and followed it up with study from books. Louis, who used to play violin with a local orchestra, works from basic songs which Raymond puts down on tape, and aims at really using the orchestra to full instead of just as a sustained backing as often happens. Completing the Froggatt group are drummer Len Ablethorpe and guitarist Hartley Cane who possesses a remarkable instrument he built himself—an 18-string guitar. Twelve strings are tuned in the conventional 12-string manner, plus six banjo strings tuned to the octave of the high strings.

Broadcasting

The Raymond Froggatt group are currently doing quite a bit of broadcasting with the Des Champ Orchestra, as well as reverting to what they used to do—folk, early Dylan and instrumentals. Raymond himself is a successful songwriter, having composed Cliff Richard's hit *Big Ship*, and *Red Balloon* which took the Dave Clark Five into the charts.

But the main aim is to expand on the work with orchestra, to show people what really goes into strings. As this expands, the gap between pop and classical music may well narrow, and no doubt new ideas will spring up, as more young people become aware of orchestras. We had one for a start as we talked: how about an orchestral concert along with the pop groups in Hyde Park?   M.H.

12

60

Chapter five

TERRY KENNEDY

Our families were very thrilled about us getting a record contract and we, likewise, couldn't wait to present them with a record which bore our name.

We were expected in Polydor's office in Stratford Place, Oxford Street, London at 11.00 o'clock the following Monday to sign the contracts. At 9.00 o'clock we were sitting outside in the van for someone to arrive, so keen to sign our lives away. We hadn't got a manager and no thought of negotiating for percentages or time options entered our heads. Polydor could have signed us up for the rest of our lives and paid us nothing. It turned out that it was a standard recording contract with five percent royalty payment for a period of five years, all recording costs to be recouped from our royalty payments. Unlike today, groups had no desire to deal. We just wanted to make records. In fact we were taking the business at face value. We were bound to get hurt, but in doing so we early bands paved the way for today's musicians to be very careful in their negotiations. They now know, because of our experience, that this business bites and if you are not sharp it will swallow you too, right down to your boots; but more of that later.

Fortunately for us our five years with Polydor were to be some of the happiest of our career. We were going to learn all aspects of recording and meet people of all sorts; good, bad and some who we still work with, who will remain lifelong friends.

We entered the offices feeling very small and insignificant. The reception area was decked out with Gold Albums; mostly with the Atlantic label on them. Atlantic Records were Polydor's American operators. This was the big time and we knew it. A very beautiful girl invited us to follow her into the inner office area. We shuffled after her, feeling and looking very stupid. The girl knocked a very official looking door. The knock had prompted a loud utterance of 'Come'. We four looked at each other, I think for support more than anything else, and I noticed that we had unconsciously formed a line abreast of each other. It occurred to me at that moment that we looked like four escapees from Rampton. We were all dying to laugh.

We were greeted from behind the huge desk by a tall slim man. He had slightly protruding teeth which gave him a very friendly reassuring smile. His thick-rimmed spectacles and silver-grey hair depicted the perfect gentleman. His skin had that buffed rich look w h i c h complimented his perfectly cut slate blue suit. As we stood before him we must have looked like four used Brillo pads. 'I am Roland Rennee, and I am the Managing Director here. I  have heard all about you from my spies', he laughed, I imagine to put us at our ease. I noticed two or three flies had begun to dive-bomb Lou, but he was doing his best to ignore them. 'I am told that you have hit record potential and I'm sure that you're going to be successful with us'. He gave us the contracts to sign and we all signed them without reading them. Then he told us to go home and wait to hear from him. Their plan was to put us with a good producer in the studio as soon as possible. He shook our hands and bade us farewell, telling us how nice, and what a great pleasure it was to meet us. We all liked Roland. We believed that he really was pleased to meet us. The next five years were to teach us a great deal about the workings of the entertainment world and the people who cut and slash about within it, some like great cruel blades disguised as soft sympathetic pillows, willing to bite the heads from the unsuspecting and weary. Their cunning is as real as fire and their compassion as rare as gold. They will take your natural kindness, screw it into a ball and boot it to the moon, and if you fall in pieces they will call you litter. We were to become worms among worms, writhing within each other's slime in order to breathe. Lies, delivered with smiles, will baffle good minds and if your misguided feet step into enough bullshit you will begin to smell of failure. We were to learn how to treasure our spirit and never to forget our reason for being there. The music business is like a great grey sculpture carved out of granite. From many angles it is difficult to see what it is supposed to be; but if you stand the right distance away and view it from the front, imagine the blue aura of goodness which is abundant within it, and if you listen for the strains of marvellous melody which is created be cause of it, then it can look stunningly beautiful.

We were to be kicked by this new grey master many times. We would yelp and cower and, like forgiving dogs, wag our tails and return to its feet at the first whistle. We might be called foolish, but how could we believe that something we loved so much would really want to hurt us. We have never been cry-babies and we are as tough as they come. The proof of this is the fact that we are still here after twenty years, muscle-bound and laughing.

A week passed and we received our first package from Polydor Records It contained a demonstration disc of a song written and performed by an Australian band called 'The Bee Gees'. They were an unknown band brought to Polydor's attention by a man called Robert Stigwood. Their success together was to become legendary throughout the whole world. The accompanying note informed us that we were required to learn the song and be at the office in London three days later to meet our first producer.

The song was entitled 'The House of Lords'. The Bee Gees performance of this piece was in a definite Beatles style, with two part harmony encompassing the whole of the lyric. We found this very disconcerting as the style was completely out of character with the direction we had hoped to follow. Because of our inexperience however, we didn't think of rearranging the song to suit us, so we copied the demo recording note for note in the hope that we wouldn't offend anyone who had chosen the song for us to record.

Our arrival in London was on a summer's day. We were four hours early. Parked in Stratford Place, we watched two men erect a striped canopy at the doorway of an office block opposite Polydor's building. We didn't have any money to do anything civilised, like going for a coffee, so we just sat and waited. We were nervous but happy. My young, hopeful friends and I, among millions of others, had something to do that day. Why was it that everyone who passed by seemed to moved with knowledge of direction, at such speed, whilst we tripped and stumbled through these hours?

The staff at Polydor's office began to arrive at 10.30; our appointment was set for 11.00 o'clock. As we wandered into the reception area it was comforting to be greeted by the same girl whom we had met on our first visit. Even more comforting was the fact that she was expecting us, and immediately led us to the small recording studio situated in the same building. After being told to set up our equipment, she asked us if we would like coffee. We were then told that the Producer would be arriving shortly.

It seems to me that nightmares, illness, accidents and personal stupidity can rock your life, sometimes throwing you to the ground and sometimes changing your steady contented mind, but all these things, although distracting, are usually brought under control, and fitted in to your steady mind's unchangeable direction. Although the application of yourself into life may be slightly different, you will remain essentially yourself.

Such is the invasion of the inanimate trespass. Not so, the invasion of some people to which our steady minds have no control at all. We either dislike or dismiss, or we welcome and accept. Sometimes, because of knowing them, we will prosper and sometimes we will fall. At the worst we can fall apart in despair and kill. At best we will learn, and find complete love. There are those who enter your life and completely stop your chain of thought; alter your destiny and shape your future path, simply because you want them to be always there. In some cases how fortunately vulnerable we are to succumb to this simple form of need for each other.

Terry Kennedy walked into our world through the wrong door. We had set up our equipment at the far end of the studio, facing the entrance from which we thought he would appear. He came from behind and was among us before we had noticed. He was to remain as unpredictable as he was brilliant throughout the rest of our association which was to last for five years.

To try to describe Terry to anyone is like throwing sand into the wind; some grains will fly forward and some will fly back, but the grains look exactly the same. There was nothing one could say about him that seems to fit his personality. His enthusiasm for this business was total. He reminded me of a catherine wheel; commanding everyone's attention whilst spinning on a post; but if he broke free to spin wildly on the floor, people would kick and stamp in an attempt to put him out, in the fear of getting burned. Everyone who knew him loved his controlled flair. He just never found a strong enough nail to spin on. I have to write about him with the knowledge that he is now dead. I know that if I wrote this without conviction and complete honesty, he would consider me unprofessional and be disappointed with me. That would never do whilst he lived, and he taught me too much for me to change now he is dead.

When we met Terry he was dressed in grey slacks, black slip-on shoes, a pink shirt and a grey and black striped jacket. He had black curly hair and wore Buddy Holly type glasses. He was very slim and stooped slightly forward. As he talked his fingers would be constantly fidgeting around his shirt collar. He wrestled with everything that was said to him and everything he said to you, in order to wring laughter from whosever company he happened to be in.

'I'm Terry Kennedy and this is Lisa', he introduced us to his very nice secretary who was to become one of our greatest fans. 'I will be producing your first record, so let me hear you play and sing it, and then we will go for a drink'. We were pretty confident as we ran through the song. Terry listened without interruption. His only comment when we finished was 'You have a great voice Froggie, I think one day we will have a hit'.

'Right, let's go for that drink'. We were surprised that he did not want to hear more from us but ours is not to reason why. As we followed him down South Moulten Street I explained that we were broke and could not buy a drink. He said that Polydor were not broke and that they owed us a few drinks - his expense account would take care of it. In the bar of the South Moulten Pub it became clear that he wanted to introduce himself to us more fully, and also get to know us more as people. As we were to work together very closely, knowledge of each other, to his mind, was essential.

He told us that he had discovered Donovan and produced his hits, 'Catch the Wind' and 'Colours', and also he had produced all the Ivy League's hits. We were very impressed and felt very privileged to be involved with him. Our pedigree on the other hand seemed rather dull, but he listened to our ideas and our hopes; giving us a new status with his warm interest. He explained to us the almost impossible chance of picking up a hit song from an outside writer, whose publishers would always approach the major established artistes with anything that had the quality of being successful. It was vital that we tried to create a hit song of our own. His point was taken, but we weren't sure our own ability to achieve this mammoth task. We would, however, try.

Being unexpectedly booked into the Hyde Park Towers Hotel was a nice surprise for us. We were given some expenses by Polydor Records and we spent the next day rehearsing with Terry at a real rehearsal room in the West End. It was really strange to work with a producer. We were having to play and sing his ideas instead of our own. We found it very refreshing and Terry could see capabilities in us we never knew existed. He began, there and then to dig out our unused talent. It was like having a mental massage.

The following morning at 10.30 am we arrived at Advision Recording Studio in New Bond Street. We were about to embark on the first proper professional engagement we had ever had. I'm sure I don't have to tell you that we all felt terrific!

From left to right, Roger, Frogs cusion Golly Froggatt

It surprised us to find some other musicians there but Terry explained that he wanted two drummers playing, and an extra acoustic guitar. Don't forget we only had four track recording desks in those days, so multitracking was a long complicated business, resulting in vast studio costs and if you were not an established band these large budgets were not made available to you. Therefore it was cheaper and more sensible to hire session musicians, thus overcoming the problem of time and money consuming over-dubs.

It took us all day and most of the night to complete the record and Terry was his usual enthusiastic self throughout the whole proceedings. I am bound to say that I did not like the record at all, in fact it used to, and still does, embarrass me whenever I hear it. Anyway, the recording company liked it and it was released. Thankfully, it did not get any airplay, so it never did us any damage. In fact, it did us a lot of good because we knew we could do better and our relationship with Terry was cemented. We also felt that we could write a better song that the one the Bee Gees wrote for us. I think we were feeling for the first time that we belonged in this business and that we at last had something to contribute. I had been writing songs for the band's performance but had never written a song for us with a recording in mind. This task was decidedly different. A single record song, in those days, couldn't last for more than two and a half to three minutes and, with no local radio stations, we all had to aim for Radio One, and their strict needle time problem made them very choosy indeed. Therefore inside three minutes a song had to repeat its hook line as many times as possible without sounding repetitive, and also have a story verse in a commercial modern style, which could be memorised easily. This is called construction. In pop songs it is as vital as the creative mind. Construction isn't part of the art, but if it is done badly then you will miss your market and, more importantly, you will miss the point of popular music, which is - don't get fancy, just get up there'.

I have always had a great love for music of all kinds and so for me to be attempting to write a song for us to record was very exciting indeed. My biggest problem was that I couldn't play an instrument of any kind, so I had to create everything in my head and then try to explain to the boys how the tune and feel of the work sounded verbally. Because of this handicap my songs have always been simple three-chord efforts. I think perhaps that this has been their appeal to the many people who have found pleasure in them over the years. On the other hand, lyric writing comes completely natural to me. I cannot be pretentious because I'm not that clever, so all my works are true, and all people must have experienced everything I write about. Their hearts have only ever been a word away from me, so I'm fortunately able to touch someone I don't know, just because they are the same as me.

A month passed and our record, The House of Lords, had not done any business at all - but Polydor and Terry Kennedy had faith in us to eventually produce the goods.

Terry rang us to see if we had any songs for him to listen to. I had written three. These were; 'We're All Going to the Seaside', 'Somethin's Going On', and 'Red Balloon'. He asked us all to come down to London and have a day with him so that he could hear them. We suggested that we could meet the following day and he agreed. 'Ten o'clock in the morning at Polydor Records - I'll see you there'. He rang off, and the same apprehension I had felt many times before and since, returned.

'Don't bother to set your gear up - just play the songs to me on acoustic guitar with one voice'. Out of respect - although rather puzzled - we obeyed. We hadn't learned yet that it is easier for a producer to judge a song if it has not been arranged. Feeling a little self-conscious I began to sing my song, with H. Cain strumming the guitar. The next few moments were going to launch us into the music industry like a bullet.

I had explained that the song was about children playing in a park in France, with a verse written in French just for good measure to give it that little bit of difference. H. Cain struck a chord:

In and out of the red balloon
Marry the farmer's daughter
Sleepy heads in the afternoon
Callow-la-callow-la-vita.

Terry's face began to change. His eyes were becoming wider and a happy sort of frown appeared.

The old man passed me by
And he didn't hear me cry
And I never knew his name
And he never came again.

Terry was by now visibly shaking. The catherine wheel was beginning to spin. We hadn't seen him like this before and he was beginning to excite us.

And the sun was coming out
And the kids began to shout
And the dogs began to bark
In the lovely Paris park.

In and out of the Red Balloon
Marry the farmer's daughter
Sleepy heads in the afternoon
Callow-la-callow-la-vita.

'Stay there', Terry disappeared for a few moments. Len said 'I think he likes it'. He was a master of the understatement! Terry returned with four office girls. 'Play it again - listen to this, then tell me what you think. You'll love it'. They loved it - they hadn't any choice. Terry was instant fire. He disappeared again and came back with Roland Rennee. 'Play it again'. We did, and Roland said 'Go in and record it. Well done lads'.

We had played Red Balloon first because we thought it was the weakest song of the three, but Terry knew something that we didn't dare dream about. 'That song will sell millions of copies all over the world'. He was dead right. God bless him! He didn't want to hear the other two songs. 'They will do for later, let's go for a drink. By the way,' he enquired 'What does Callow-la-vita mean?" 'It's broken French for how warm life is', I answered. 'You'd better believe it Froggie, you'd better believe it'.

Chapter six

STUART REID

A small sharp man stepped into the Advision Recording Studio. New Bond Street, the studio where the Moody Blues had recorded 'Go Now' and the Move made their classic hit 'I Can Hear The Grass Grow', the same studio where we were about to record our second attempt at the charts. He was about 50 years old, dressed in an immaculate navy blue suit, a pink shirt, white tie and black slip on shoes. A very striking, expensive looking fellow indeed. Terry introduced to us to Stuart Reid, a music publisher from E. H. Morris Music Corporation I liked him immediately. We became, and still are, great friends. He listened to 'The Red Balloon' and two other songs I had written, and declared then that he would like to become my publisher. I was pleased, but not too excited, because I didn't know what that meant exactly, and anyway I was still over the moon about making records. As he was leaving he told me he would draw up an agreement and be in touch with us very soon. We thanked him, expressed how nice it was to meet him, and said goodbye, and continued to record the backing rhythm track to 'The Red Balloon'.

Terry Kennedy then employed an arranger by the name of Phil Dennis, who was one of the hottest arrangers at the time. One of his works was Number 1 in the chart of the day; 'Cinderella Rockafella'. His next job was to orchestrate 'The Red Balloon' for us. He made a superb effort and the finished record was a classic piece of Sixties music.

So, with Terry Kennedy the Producer, Stuart Reid the Publisher, Raymond Froggatt the artiste and Polydor Records the Label, 'The Red Balloon' was released on the second Friday in June 1968. Our band had been formed for almost six years. 'The Red Balloon' was played on every radio show, every day for two months. All of the Radio One and Radio Two producers loved it. Surely nothing could stop us having our first hit record now?

We were soon to learn the folly of not having a manager with front and power to get things moving. This lack of push from our side resulted in almost non-existent distribution to the retailers. Polydor were a young company in England and they hadn't quite got their act together. Even with sale or return from retailers, which doesn't exist now, they failed to get the record into the shops.

The result was that our lovely record, 'The Red Balloon', was dead. I felt the first pain of professional disappointment. My world seemed to collapse. You see we didn't mind the failure of our first record, because it wasn't up to scratch, but this was different.

My young friends and I took that disappointment with the same spirit which had kept us going for six years. We only hoped that Terry and Stuart would feel the same way. We need not have worried. They were as strong as us. In fact they felt that we had made a giant step forward.

We had to be careful with our follow-up record, because even though our 'Red Balloon' missed, we had made quite an impact with the media, and our next offering was awaited with a great deal of interest.

Dave Clark was driving home late one night listening to the radio, when the DJ announced the next record; 'The Red Balloon' by Raymond Froggatt. The first verse had played and Dave stopped his car to make a note of the title and record label. This great star's late night journey was to help me become one of the happiest songwriters in the world.

I had a call from Stuart Reid inviting me and the band out to dinner one evening. He had some good news for us, and we could also meet his wife. He suggested the Old Vienna restaurant in Bond Street. We were going to experience the joy of proper dining, as opposed to just feeding at a table. Seven o'clock at the South Moulten Pub, we eagerly awaited the arrival of Stuart and his wife. There was me, Lou, Len and H. Cain, all tarted up, drinking halves of lager, about to dine in London's West End with a top publisher and his wife. We had come a long way from sharing a bag of chips in the back of an old van. We were still skint, but now with a touch of class.

H. Cain, Len Abelthorpe, Frog & Lou Clark

Patsy was lovely. A very kind face, which confounded any unfortunate person's misapprehensions that she would tell you anything other than exactly what was on her mind. Indeed, when I asked her what she thought of our music, she said 'Well, you sound like a bunch of hill-billies to me'. Having moved over to the Country music of our business now that many years have passed, it looks as if she was dead right.

We dined in many places all over London after that first night, we became very accomplished diners, ordering all manner of cuisine. A nice part of our fantastic adventure!

Dave Clark's version of 'The Red Balloon' reached the top five in the charts. I was now a hit song writer. Again you see the folly of not having a Manager. We could not capitalise on this success because we didn't know what to do. Here we were with a world star in the charts, with one of our songs, and our version of the same song in every chart in Europe. The song reached number one in France recorded by one of France's top stars, Marie Laforet. 'The Red Balloon' was recorded by over sixteen other artists all over the world. Almost immediately I wrote a song called 'Big Ship' for Lulu, and the Eurovision Song Contest Panel turned it down. Mickey Most was Lulu's Manager at the time and he was convinced 'Big Ship' was a hit song. In those days Mickey Most was always right. Stuart decided to try the song with Peter Noon. Sadly, as with all songs, they don't suit everybody. It didn't work. Mickey had talked about the song in the Melody Maker. His comments were always highly thought of. Cliff Richard's Management picked the song up. Cliff then recorded it. The

song became a world hit and I had written my second hit song. You can see the luck; those little bits of hope scattered everywhere for everyone, remember?

Here we were then, a band with two hit songs, a five year recording contract, a five year publishing contract, a top line record producer, records in every chart in Europe, and not a clue how to use this good fortune in order to further our careers. We really did do it for the music. This business was going to get harder and more painful but we didn't know it. There was the first crack of decay forming somewhere within us but none of us could see it. Mental changes; natural physical growth; shadows of individual serious thought; personal time with other people; those other people's opinions; different roads; my friends were becoming men. I knew for the first time that one day they would all fly away. When you fly my dears, God's speed, God's speed.

$\mathcal{C}$hapter seven

1972 AND CHANGES

The following four years with Polydor Records helped us to understand fully the inner workings of our industry. We made some of our best and worst records. We made friendships with people who were just like us. Some became world famous and some fell away from the sheer frustration of it all.

Even though these times were new and, in many ways, thrilling for the band, the lack of commercial success was beginning to hurt Terry Kennedy deeply. He was drinking two bottles of bourbon a day and there were times when we feared for him greatly. He began to lose his incredible magic, the individual style of production that exploded from his mind was somehow greying. His brightness met winter and was fading. I could seem him becoming cold and indifferent to his days. He had such faith in us. To this day I feel responsible that I couldn't find the song we needed to make it all happen for us.

Our contract with Polydor came to an end. Roland Rennee had parted company with them two years earlier. The Company had lost confidence in Terry, so there was no one there who thought us worth signing for a further term.

Our time with Polydor was over. Terry Kennedy left the country to work in the Swedish music industry. We were older, wiser, and right back were we started.

At this point we had to assess what we had achieved since we had been with Polydor Records. Our second board meeting took place in a pub in Stratford upon Avon. We had all decided through the years to settle there. All of the boys had met their future wives and had already, or were about to marry. H. Cain lived with his wife in Bidford on Avon. Len and Lou lived next door to each other in their new houses in Stratford. I had my home in a small village called Wootten Wawen nearby.

Here we were then, at the Slug and Lettuce, Stratford upon Avon. I even remember the first round; two pints of bitter - H. Cain and Lou Clark, one whisky - old fashioned and lager - Len Ablethorpe, and one whisky and large coke for yours truly.

It's quite incredible to me that we, who are day by day thinkers, can look back over four years and find the amazing amount of movement we make in our lives. Some of the movement is forward, and some of it back. Some for the better, some to regret. Pride in some, shame in another, but movement all the same.

We had moved so far forward it astonished us. We talked of our twelve Polydor single record releases, all of them made in the best studios of the time. Our lovely album 'The Voice' and 'Writings', our songs had been world hits by the biggest artistes in the industry, our remarkable rise from van dwellers to West End invited diners. How important it is to know the DJs and producers of the BBC. We knew them all by name and everyone of those illustrious people liked us. We had worked in television all over Europe. The young unknown Dave Lee Travis and us on the great German TV rock show called 'Beat Club'. Admittedly we did have to give the producer the fee back, but it was a great experience. Everything has to be paid for, but every paid for thing is most certainly invaluable experience. We were the only band in the country who could perform with an orchestra - and we did too! Four times, all our own music, all orchestrated and conducted by our own bass player.

We still had our contract with Stuart Reid for the publishing of our songs. Just because Polydor had said goodbye it was certain that others would love to say hello. Let's knock on their doors!

The more we assessed ourselves, the more of a nonsense Len's opening statement, 'Well! What the **** are we going to do now then?" seemed to be.

Drink now, London tomorrow. We were more serious at this time in our lives, but we were great friends and we never found it hard to laugh at any misfortune. Good men, gallant friends, we have got to start all over again. We are stronger now, we know more now. We are better at what we do now. We know all of the dangers now. We can't be hurt again. Can we?

Stuart Reid hadn't been idle. He had been sounding recording companies out for a long time before our Polydor contract had expired. Publishers sometimes do get involved to this extent on behalf of an artiste, especially if, like us, the artiste hasn't any management.

There had been lots of interest shown by big companies, but we chose to sign with Bell Records. They were an American company with a new office in London. Dick Leahy was the head man, and we liked him. He told me he would like one single and an album in our first year. Our contract was for three years. Our next problem was to find a new record producer.

This was not quite as easy as it seems. Producers come in all shades of colour. Some are the whole rainbow, some are deep and blue, some are grey and boring, all are original in their approach. The snag is, finding one who can be in sympathy with what you are trying to do. To help you without changing you. One who can love your music but remain objective to its construction.

A tremendous crack appeared within our band. I could sense it. Something was wrong. It wasn't the industry, it was closer to us than that. A mind was pulling at the invisible chain that bound us. The day had arrived. One of us wanted to take another road. A road with more loyalty? Honesty? Friendship? A road with fonder memories? Of course not! It is someone else's road, a road they must follow to be true to themselves. Remember their dreams are just as important as ours could ever be. I understand Lou, I only want you to find your piece of time. I only want you to show the world how great you are. You are great you know! Four years at Leeds College of Music to brush up on your choral and orchestral talents my God Lou, you will be dynamite at the end of that! Good luck my dear friend. Don't ever change, and if ever you need me, I ain't hard to find. Bye Lou, take care.

Stuart Reid was disappointed. He wondered how our new record company would take the news. To lose someone as good as Lou was quite a blow, but Lou would be the first to say that anyone can be replaced in music, because he knows that in our hearts he will always be there.

We found a player almost immediately. We offered a very attractive place, and it was filled by Mick Hinks. He had played in a soul and blues band from Birmingham called 'Locomotive', a rock band called 'The Dog That Bit People', and when he joined us he was in the 'John Alan Duo'. Len had known him before and I was introduced to him in the Three Tuns pub in Henley-in-Arden. It's really strange how most of the milestones in my life seem to have been in pubs!

Anyway, I liked Mick. He was a great player and a very funny guy indeed. He was younger than us, so here was an injection of joyful youth.

He was so happy about his new future. Now we had to make a single and an album. I had composed the songs already, so, producer come forth - we are ready for you.

Left to Right Len Abelthorpe, Lou Clark, Frog, H. Cain on Frog's fence in Warwickshire.

Chapter eight

BELL, BAIN AND BLEACH

You might think that my next decision has to rate as one of the most daring and stupid in the history of popular music, and I'm bound to say that at the time I felt more than a little apprehensive. The reason for me to come to this decision was anything but commonsense, because advice from the lead singer of Black Sabbath at 11 o-clock in a Birmingham pub leaves very little in the shape of commonsense, uncommonsense, or sense in any shape or form.

Ozzy Osbourne was in town and called for me to go for a light ale. What a wonderful sense of understatement the dear boy has. His idea of a light ale would refloat Atlantis! Why not go for a drink with Ozzy? He is great company and I needed a good laugh. 'How are you doing Oz'? He'd just finished his album and was out to celebrate. None of the Sabbath band would go out with him - I wonder why? He was telling me about the recording of his album, when he gave a gigantic sneeze. A great piece of cabbage shot down his nose on to the table. After informing me that he had eaten it for lunch, he promptly ate it again, saying how expensive food was in London! It reminded him that he had taken lunch with the producer of his album, before he got the train back home. 'Roger Bain - he's great' said Ozzy, 'you should have him for your album'. This was surely a sign from God. How can you ignore a piece of cabbage shooting out of the nose of the maddest singer in the world? A piece of cabbage that reminded him of a producer who had just completed an album of music that could not be further away from my style. I had to meet Roger Bain because of a piece of notralistically regurgitated brassica, our band made one the finest produced albums you will hear. Good on ya Oz!

Roger Bain worked for Hummingbird Productions. He had a great reputation for his producing talent, and also for being a great guy. We first met him in Stuart Reid's office in Bond Street. E. H. Morris, my first Publisher, had been sold to Chappell Music. I automatically became a Chappell Music writer, and Stuart was now the head of Chappell. Roger wanted to hear a song so that he could judge if he could be spiritually involved. I sang to him 'The Singer'. He wanted to record it straight away. We had found our new Producer.

Bell Records our new label, Roger Bain our new Producer, Mick Hinks our new bassist, and 'Bleach' our new album. Here we go again kids! Hold tight, it's bound to get bumpy. If we get tossed about too much we can get off and rest a bit. If the storm gets too rough we will shelter beneath the rock of our courage. If the thunder is too loud we can pretend it's a drumbeat. If we feel we could cry we will disguise tears with violins. If our strength should desert us then we will lean on our friendship. If our pockets grow thin, then our songs will sustain us. For all that is ours will be free and among us.

We used Trident recording studio to make 'Bleach'. Our single, 'The Singer', would be part of the same sessions. Elton John had just finished his classic track, 'Your Song', at the same studio. We all knew that it would be a monster hit classic. Good old Reg!

It was a great experience making 'Bleach'. We had open-ended time in the studio, and an unlimited budget, but we were never silly in the studio. Time is very precious, not only from the money point of view, but from the very real danger that the longer you spend in there, the more chance you have of getting sound-drunk. You or your engineer and the producer will become indifferent and bored - you will have no record then. You must try to keep vital, and create an air of joy. The more you care about recording, the better you will like your song and, if you like it, other people might as well. You never know.

The whole atmosphere of our world was changing. We liked this new thing better. When I look back, I suppose it was the Sixties leaving as the Seventies arrived. Music was changing. I liked the change. It refreshed me to see something new. I loved the Sixties of course, but you can't drag music about, it lives in people's hearts. We must always try to create more. It's healthy, why shouldn't we enjoy a new song when we are eighty. Why must the song be as old as us! Our minds are new as the morning we wake. I hold all I've heard in my memory, and I think of what I have heard when I am alone.

A young man's morning is my morning too, so it's my right, as it's his, to hear something new.

Roger Bain was a revelation to us. It's true we had a lot of knowledge of studio recording, but he showed us the way to use our abilities and marry them to the new technology, how to make the most of multitrack recording, the use of sound tracks for atmosphere. He worked with H. Cain so perfectly to bring out his natural flair for arrangements. These sessions resulted in a fine bunch of recordings that still stand up to day for the standard of production.

'The Singer' was released, and was well received by the media. It had an unfortunate airing though. Rosco played it on his Round Table programme at the speed of 78 rpm. It sounded like Pinky and Perky. He let it play until the end like that, because he said it was too slow. There was much mirth among the panelists, and my song received an unfair low blow. Rosco later apologised to me at the BBC after Cliff Richard had recorded it, and he claimed in the Press that it was his favourite song. I sent Rosco a speeded up version of Colonel Bogie. He never responded.

We had a Top of the Pops appearance with 'The Singer'. It was the only song that week that didn't hit the charts, but it was worth doing, because that day I met and became friends with the great Marc Bolan. He and his wife Gloria were terrific people. I loved them both and miss them always.

'Bleach' was released, and acclaimed by the Press, and our peers, as one of the top ten albums of all time. Rolling Stone magazine referred to 'Bleach' as an outstanding example of British music. Today the album is fetching ú100 on the rare record market.

At this time Cliff Richard was recording one song after another, and one day I had an opportunity to meet him. I was invited to Abbey Road studio to witness a session of Cliff recording my songs. Can you imagine what that must have been like? The great man at work and I had supplied him with the songs. I was speechless! I spent the whole day with Cliff. We became, and still are, great friends. I went out to dinner with him when he came to Birmingham. It was a really posh restaurant. As we sat down it was obvious that everyone was looking at him. He just leaned over to me and said 'I bet you they are all saying who's that bloke sitting with Froggie'? Love ya! Cliff.

Our concert schedule at this period of time was formidable. Admittedly, we did travel in a more civilised manner. If we now had to go to Germany, Yugoslavia or France. We would fly. We were always met by representatives from whatever TV programme we were appearing on, and treated like proper human beings. I have always felt the need to respond to attitudes of indifference. I will never allow anyone who is professionally connected with me to be derided in any way. I don't mean by this that we should be treated like Lords. On the contrary, we are kids from the streets, but most of us are professional artistes. The reason that we arrive at a venue is presumably because we are part of the show. If we are part of the support for that show none of us artistes expect the same billing, or the same money. What we do expect however is a polite greeting and adequate facilities to wash and change. Remember some of us have usually travelled hundreds of miles to get there. I have known promoters to provide none of these basic professional needs, and then have the audacity to slander the band for being in need of a wash and change. The utter contempt of these people disgusts me. I call them the Broom Cupboard Brigade, because that's where they expect us to spend our time.

The first year into our Contract with Bell Records was probably one of our busiest years. We had made two singles and two albums, the second of which has never been released. The title is 'Handle With Care'. I really enjoyed making that one because it was recorded at Island Studio. This magnificent place was used by all the big stars and their engineers were, as they are today, first class. I'll explain why this album wasn't released later.

At this time I had signed us up to an agency called 'Starlite Artistes'. The Company's big groups were the

Tremeloes and the Marmalade. We toured with both of them all over Europe. This episode was a kind of miscasting for us. I was beginning to feel a little lost. Our recording company was successful with the Bay City Rollers and Gary Glitter. Our agents were working us with absolute 'dyed in the cloth' pop bands. I could sense us losing our identity. It was hurting us and I didn't know why. I had no one to help me make my decisions. It was because of me and my ignorance of the inner industry, that all of my anchors were set adrift. All of my talented friends and our crazy dreams would begin to fall apart. My friends were growing into their own lives while I was shrinking into darkness, foolishness, and instead of dreams I began to chase hopes. I was an ambitious fool running at my own pace, instead of the natural pace of mankind.

Chapter nine

DON ARDEN AND JET RECORDS

For many years I considered my next move to be the most damaging of my career; but with the passing of time, and the movement of the hours, hindsight, experience, knowledge, and plain dogged work, I'm now not so sure. Very few people from my background could have the opportunity to feel the real pleasure and excitement the next few years would show to me. I will try to portray this time to you without malice or vengeance. You see I believe that everyone is blameless for the sometimes necessary in-fighting that goes on. It's just part and parcel of this incredible industry. To be creative and keep the instinct of professional survival seems almost impossible to comprehend, but the creativity and struggles are there. Sometimes people get hurt, it's true. On the other hand sometimes people receive magnificent rewards for their efforts. Who is there to say who deserves to succeed or fail? The first day I sang I only wanted people to listen. The first song I wrote - I only hoped the people could understand. People's ears and understandings I now have. So you see, I am a success. My heart is still whole, my spirit is high, my mind is in tune, and my songs are simple. I can live with all things, and I still find myself a stranger, yet I dream the same pictures as you. I have been given a great gift of friendship by people I have never met, but I know you my dears in music. I really do.

Don Arden is the most dynamic, charismatic, forthright, gutsy, fearless, knowledgeable, hardworking, amusing dangerous, music industry legend I have ever known. Immensely likeable, but as stern and unpredictable as the sea. He could knock the spirit out of a charging bull elephant with a single stare. His success with world stars is beautifully daunting. Almost all of the artistes who have arrived at his office for the first time were skint. Almost all of them (having achieved world acclaim) then ungratefully arrive at court to sue him in a Rolls Royce. They always lost. Love him or hate him, take it from me Don Arden is a great man!

My association with Don began after a conversation with Roy Wood. Roy knew my contract with Bell was almost over and my publishing agreement with Chappell Music was about to expire. I was flattered when Roy had told me that Don had shown an interest in signing me for recording and publishing. I knew of Don's reputation for making people successful, and his great power in the industry impressed me. I thought that this opportunity would give us the best chance of making it as a band, also, I have always had a great respect for Roy Wood. The thought of being part of the same stable as him and Jeff Lynn put stars in my yes. You see, even people as experienced as I was then, are still suckers when a promise is made for them to finally reach their dream. Stuart Reid had no idea at the time that I was thinking of making a move to another publishing house. As my Agreement with Chappell Music had almost reached its full term he made an offer of £30,000 non-returnable advance to sign a new contract with Chappell Music for a further five years. This Agreement would have given the Company sole rights to the copyright of my songs in this period for life, for every territory in the world. This was a very generous offer, and not unusual in those days. Don't forget I had written two world hits, and many songs for Cliff. At this time I was considered to be a very valuable song writing property, and most major publishing houses would have signed me up immediately.

I turned this offer down. Stuart Reid was professionally disappointed, and absolutely personally dreadfully hurt. He begged me to reconsider, but the pull of a different direction was too strong for me. The Don Arden set up looked like a chance for me to get to America. I just couldn't resist the challenge. A chance, surely everyone takes a chance.

Every day is littered with people who never took a chance and lost, while others win. It never stops us though; it's the human condition. We leap in and out of fire all of our lives, and if commonsense came into it I suppose we would all still be cavemen. Anyway, commonsense is a luxury in the music industry. Very few of us are blessed with it, that is why we are so vulnerable. I don't think this lack of commonsense makes us fools. We are just barmy minstrels singing and playing to shadows of hope.

Well, I'll tell you, what a road to travel; unsurfaced, no cat's eyes, bends everywhere, no warning signs, problems coming at you like juggernauts, and all of us at some time are riding that road without insurance. You don't get insurance on Music Road, but I don't know anyone who has regretted being on it. If nothing else, it's a great teacher, and there are many wonderful stops along the way.

My first meeting with Don Arden was like colliding head on with a train. His presence was riveting. Here I was, talking to a real mogul. He had confidence in every sinew of his being. This was the first time I had been in the company of a music businessman who could not have cared less about being friends with anyone. He has so much knowledge and all the bottle you need to go with it.

I had just turned down £30,000 and the fact that he wanted to sign me up for absolutely nothing seemed like a better deal. I couldn't wait to get involved, so I signed. The act of a madman? Well, see what you think later.

Jet Records had not been formed yet, and the ELO was still in its embryo stage. Roy Wood had formed Electric Light Orchestra, and involved Jeff Lynn as a songwriter/player.

For some reason there had been an internal problem in ELO I have to say I won't comment on the finer points of the rift because it is Roy and Jeff's personal business. I couldn't presume to betray their private affairs. You wouldn't want me to anyway.

90

The ELO was handed over to Jeff Lynn, and Roy Wood formed Wizzard. Don's Company was called Dartbill. It's difficult to say what the Company's actual function was, but Roy, Jeff and Frog were signed to it. I don't know if it was the same for the others, but my publishing was signed to Dartbill, as was my record-making future. As far as I can make out, Don Arden then sold my publishing to a major publishing house for an advance payment of many thousands of pounds. I was now a writer for Robbins EMI Music Publishers. My future recordings were sold before they were made, to Warner Bros in the same fashion. I didn't receive any of these monies because Don had quite legally operated a Power of Attorney on my behalf through his Company. So you see, he didn't need my signature to bring these deals into operation. The same techniques were used in America where I became a writer for ATV Music. My recordings were sold to Accord Records of New York. What's in it for me you might ask. Well, quite a bit, as you will see, not in the form of finance but in the form of promotion, recording facilities, travel and terrific fun.

I have never regretted anything I have done in this business. I have always tried to play it straight and do it in the most honest way I know how. You cannot always succeed by doing things proper, you all know that, but most of the people I have met in my life still like me. How can you define success between money and love. I don't know if that is the real worthiness of a man, but it helps me in my personal life. I don't like hurting people but sometimes life gangs up on you. Decisions have to be made that seems unfair to some people. Sometimes they are unfair. All things pass. All things change. It's the nature of our industry. I have shared every pain with all of the players I have worked with.

Most of them know that, I hope.

My first single for Warner Bros was recorded at Air Studios in Oxford Street, London. This studio is owned by George Martin, the great producer of the Beatles. Our record was produced by Tony Ashton. It was a song I had written called 'French Painter'. This was a one-off association with Tony. He is a magnificent musician and writer. Some of you might remember his great song 'Resurrection Shuffle'. He was the lead member of Ashton Gardner and Dyke, one of the most successful bands of the Sixties and Seventies. Having said all that, I have to say that I didn't like the record. For my humble taste it was far too complicated. I felt the cross

rhythms within it took away the simplicity of the song. Anyway, the studio was far too clinical for me to relax. It was, for me, rather like going to the dentist every day. Don Arden kind of liked it, but he didn't leap about with joy on the first hearing, or the second. In fact, I don't think he ever did. He could listen to an ELO album which had taken a year to make, and say 'Very nice'. Another master of the understatement. Don never fell out with anyone, they always fell out with him. You see they didn't want to kill Caesar - they wanted to be him.

'French Painter' was released and forgotten almost immediately. Warner Reprise suggested we make an album and I asked Don if I could produce it. To my amazement he said for me to go ahead. I thought perhaps

I could record it at Richard Branson's new studio, The Manor, in Oxford. To my utter disbelief Don said 'Book it for a month and get started'. What an opportunity to have happened for any band. We could come off the road for a month, each of us could have a retainer wage. Not a fortune, but enough to keep us in beer and fags! Don't forget, for anyone to have 24 hours a day for one month in one of the best recording facilities to make an album of your own songs, in the height of summer, is that stuff that dreams are made of. Manor, summer, Oxfordshire, here we come with a bag full of songs.

Chapter ten

ROGUES AND THIEVES

The Manor Recording Studio belongs to Richard Branson, at that time he was only just beginning to build his present day empire. A couple of Virgin Record shops and the Manor House and studio are the very acorns from which the great Virgin organisation grew. Those two shops and the Manor House were discarded seeds. I'm sure that without Richard Branson those seeds would never have been planted. He gardened, nurtured and watered those seeds with his marvellous entrepreneurial green fingers, until they blossomed into the world famous empire we know today. Richard is one of the very few incredibly successful businessmen that springboarded from the music industry. Another is Chris Blackwell, the owner of Island Records. I knew both of them and if I had to compare them to each other I would say that Chris Blackwell is a greater fan of music than Richard, who appears to take an infinite interest in anything that moves. They are the supermen, and absolutely vital to our industry. I believe it's because of the uncertainties and insecurities, that our business bursts forth to breed all manner of people - unfortunates who lose, every corner of their lives cobwebbed with bad luck. Some fine young faces that line and yellow through over-indulgence. The wicked consequences of the dreadful mixture of frustration, fear of failure, and hard drugs. Cheaters who hang on the coat tails of the trusting, the lost who never found the right place at the right time and then ran into fat-bellied, cigar-smoking, silk-hatted society respected muggers, the sorry, sad music makers who searched for stars and found only death, the joyful golden cheer of the fortunate, the silver stages upon which they can entertain to their full capacity, the great managers who guide the talented (without a thought to promote themselves).

There are fine people around us. Cliff Richard found one of the best. Peter Gormley has managed him for years and hardly anyone outside of our industry has heard of him. The great Chris Blackwell emerged. So did Richard Branson, and we were one of his first customers.

The Manor House is set in its own beautiful grounds, very secluded and built entirely of old stone. The interior of the house is very traditional, interesting, comfortable and extremely English. We each had our own bedroom and we would dine at a set evening dinner time, seated at the 25 foot dining table with all the staff. A mixture of Sixties' hippies, very talented engineers, office girls, and a chef who had been a roadie for the Nashville Teens. The studio itself is situated in the old stables - a simply marvellous place in which to make music. We had a totally free hand to make this next album. I decided to partly use a running concept, join songs together with incidental melody. We had a chance to try all of the techniques taught to us by Terry Kennedy and Roger Bain, plus some other ideas of production we had of our own.

I had written all the songs with my ideas of musical linkage in mind. H. Cain, Len and Mick were by now very accomplished and patient studio players. There is a world of difference playing in a studio as opposed to playing in an auditorium. Some musicians are never quite able to perceive that difference, and consequently waste a great deal of time. This is a very sad phenomenon because record companies soon lose interest in the money drain. These drains are always made of people who fail to see beyond their talent. We are all (unfortunately) temporary, but money I fear is permanent. Money is the greatest bigamist of life, for it marries itself to all things. If you treat this bigamist with contempt it won't divorce you, it will simply run off with someone else, so know your time well if you expect someone else to pay for it.

Even though we were at work it would have been impossible not to feel the joy of the Manor and its lovely surroundings. A large swimming pool, the canal, and its tow-path leading to the pub. Oh dear!

Our first day at the Manor was really spent settling in and setting up the studio, getting to know our engineer and finding our way around. The day was Monday in mid-July, and the weather was as nice as it could be in England. It would remain as beautiful for the duration of our stay. We had arrived to make our first unsupervised album. For the first time we were on our own in one of the finest studios in the country, with a huge budget for one of the biggest record companies in the world, Warner Reprise. Once again, the stuff that dreams are made of, but we had to get down to serious work. No one will pay you for dreaming.

I mentioned setting up the studio. I think I should explain to those of you who are not familiar with the mechanics of recording, exactly what this means. Usually, if a band is going in to record for two days, a specification of the line up of your instrumentation and amplification would be sent to the studio staff before the session is due to take place. The studio tape operator would then prepare the microphones and place settings before the band arrives. This saves time and eases the tension, especially if the band is inexperienced and nervous. Sometimes a producer will have a favourite studio and, whoever he is recording, he will use the same format of continuity in his approach. The studio staff would know this and prepare the facility to his preference. In our case however, having never used the Manor studio before, and that this was going to be a month-long 24 hours a day project, it was impossible to measure beforehand, and so had to be played by ear on the day. There would of course rhythm tracks consisting of bass guitar and drums. These would probably be used on every song. As for the other instruments I was hoping for creative thoughts from the musicians and suggestions of added instruments as each song began to take shape. I can't have a narrow mind to creative suggestion because I am only a songwriter. My knowledge of the range and limitations of an instruments is practically nil. I can only provide the song, and sing it. I have a certain forte for the construction of a piece, but the colour and mood can only come from proper players. I had four of the best.

I had made an addition to the band by this time, a keyboard player called Dusty Miller. Although our working relationship didn't last long, his inclusion in our line-up changed my thinking. I enjoyed the space and adventure that keyboards gave to our music. Synthesizers were at their early stages, in the form of a Moog. I knew I could never change my writing style, but my songs could be adapted to this new up and coming technology. This excited me and I have used keyboards in my recordings ever since.

We began to make our contribution to Don Arden and Warner Reprise. The early stages were slow going. We planned each day's workload the night before. For instance, one day we would put H. Cain in the studio to record his many guitar, mandolin or banjo over-dubs. Sometimes there would be as many as fifteen guitars played on one song. H. played them all. H. Cain is a master at multitrack recording. He can play many different string instruments on one song and not repeat himself once. So you see, on one of H. Cain's over-dub days, the rest of us could take a day off, swimming, playing tennis, or down to the tow-path ... to the pub.

On other days H. could take a rest while one of us did our bit. We were very rarely needed all at the same time, so the project was hard, but not as heavy as it might seem. The recording contributions probably needed me least of all.

The singer's part is usually the last thing recorded. It was a joint production effort so I had lots of time to write. Because of the environment I found myself inspired and wrote songs that eventually took the place of some of the original songs especially written for the album.

The Manor is one of those places where all kinds of famous people pop in to say 'Hello', and take a drink or two. One day an old mate of mine appeared. Academically brilliant, superbly talented, intelligent to the point of embarrassment, and an absolutely, utterly, unbelievable,  incomprehensible, loveable, unchangeable, majestic father of lunatic behaviour ... enter Bonzo Dog Doo Da Band's singer, Viv Stanshall. This wonderful man's electric presence is like canned dynamite. I'll bet you can't want to open it just to see what Viv on toast tastes like. I can tell you it beats beans on, hands down. I wonder though, if it is wise to partake in this inviting intellectual feast when you are making an album for Don Arden.

Well, what do you think I did? I opened the can of course. The tin opener was the canal towpath, the toast was the local pub, and the main ingredient Viv Stanshall. Beer swilled it all down. And me? The guest at the table. Our only companion was Richard Branson's Irish wolfhound, Bootleg. He hadn't heard of Viv, so he joined us. Bootleg matched us pint for pint. I have to say though that towards closing time his canine utterances were far closer related to English language than the oft spoken drunken dialect that Viv, myself and most other musicians have perfected to the level of a university degree. I suppose to put a finer point on it we were talking absolute twaddle.

Viv had warmed himself to the noble tapster, and managed to secure the fine privilege of afters. I had to make a brief appearance at the studio just in case the boys needed me. On my return however a certain rapped out code on a secluded window would ensure my readmittance to this quite delightful departure from my normal sanity. I was in fact needed to put my stamp of approval on what had been going on in the studio. After listening to various over-dubs and discussing their purpose in the songs I had quite forgotten about Viv and Bootleg.

An hour or two had passed when a very happy, silvery-eyed Viv entered. He was completely drenched to the skin. His explanation of how he had to jump into the canal to save Bootleg was almost accepted, when the huge frame of that magnificent wolfhound appeared. He was bone dry! Viv began giggling uncontrollably and fell full arse square on to the open log fire. Steam and sparks filled the room. Viv was rescued and put into a corner to sleep. The following day he was gone and I haven't seen him from that day to this.

We were well into the album by this time and ideas for the linking of tracks were being discussed. We had all enjoyed the dawn chorus while we had been staying in this beautiful corner of the world. A far removed dawn chorus from that which us city kids had been used to. Instead of the strangled cry of asthmatic sparrows we knew from the streets of Birmingham, we could hear a symphony of bird calls, some of which we had never heard before. In order to catch this on tape we set up a microphone in the centre of the main lawn. We waited until the first bird of Manordise issued forth its heaven-composed song. This magnificent unpaid line up of feathered backing singers were completely unaware of the fact that they were being used for the benefit of the music industry. They had just joined the ranks of musicians all over the world who have not the slightest idea what is going on half of the time. The birds have the

Royal Society for the Protection of Birds. We have the Mechanical Protection Society and the Performing Rights Society. The birds' protection comes when their species is threatened. Ours are guardians of our songs. I suppose when you get right down to it the birds and most of us sing only to the glory of the day, and so I say to you 'What's wrong with that?'

> Your tired little children are homing
> Down by the rolling sea
> If I stand and sing in the moonlight
> May they stop and listen to me
> For I sing for nothing
> I sing for nothing
> Nothing at all.

We used the dawn chorus on the song called Restless Travellers, a story of two people hitch-hiking to Spain. We discovered other morning sounds as the bird track played. We could hear the breeze and leaf rustles, the darting of some creature or other, the snapping and movements of ordinary growing things. At one stage we were blessed with a mechanical and human intrusion - a lone motorcyclist passed in the distance. Not, as you might think, an annoyance, you see his entry at the end of a verse and his departure at the start of the next was in fact very moving and correct. On the final guitar note a cockerel (no doubt standing on a distant post somewhere!) heralded the start of the day, thus applauding the end of my song.

A month soon passed by in the confines of a recording studio. We were all conscious of time, and all musicians have what they consider to be their personal standard of perfection. In most cases these personal standards are very high indeed. For instance, a player's contributions (even on just a short introduction melody) are made up of many different aspects. His instrument is one of the most complicated extensions to the human body on earth, especially when it is linked to modern amplification and technological sound aids. Just to play the thing takes a lifetime of learning, then there is the phrasing, the feel, the player's own ear for perfection, and don't forget he is usually playing something that someone else has written.

All of these things have to be absolutely correct for him to be satisfied with himself. He will always know how good he is and will always want to play for you at his very best. Because of the position his contribution takes on a track, and because of his natural talent (which will always be unique) this takes time. So, on top of all these aspects there is pressure, and it is pressure that all musicians know well. Somehow they manage to cope and finish in time - God knows how, but they do.

All of the recording has been completed on the album and we had ten days and nights to mix. Every instrument on every song has its own track. In our case thirty-two pieces of recorded sounds on each song had to be mixed down from two inch wide tape to one quarter inch tape. That will be the master. The master is the tape from which the actual record will be cut. Every operation from now until the record is ready for the shops will lose some of the dynamic quality of your original recordings.

It is important therefore to compensate for these unavoidable losses while you are mixing. This is where a good engineer and a deep thinking producer are as vital as breath.

So here we are then - first mix down to the quarter inch master tape: take the master tape to the cutting studio, the master tape is then played and the sounds cut into a vinyl covered aluminium disc called the mother lacquer. The mother lacquer is taken to the pressing factory where the two metal plates are made from it. The metal plates are fixed to the press, a lump of vinyl thrown between them, and away you go. Rogues and Thieves was complete.

We were proud of our album and it was well received by Warner Reprise. Because of this Don Arden also liked it. On its first week of release it sold eight thousand copies. On some weeks these sales are enough to get you on the charts but for us, unfortunately lots of the big boys out-sold us that week. I remember Ozzy telling me that Black Sabbath's first album showed by selling two thousand five hundred copies. It's just that bit of luck you see - we all need it now and then.

Our frustrations were always within us but we never blamed each other. The boys and me had been too much respect for one another - we had be through so much together, always knowing how hard we had all tried. We put up with each other's ways. Our temperaments were worlds apart but we never spat contempt into the face of our good friendship, not ever. We were better men than that. We had travelled and learned a lot, not only about other people, but ourselves too.

We got back on the road and did some great gigs, many universities, some club dates (most of these were turning to discos by this time). The music business was changing once again. I wondered if we had another turn in us, and if we had, I wondered if the boys had the faith to take it. I hope so.

Roy Wood had taken off like a rocket with his new band, Wizzard. He seemed always to be in the studio recording one single after another. He invited me to sing on one of them - a song called Angel Fingers. I also made an appearance on Top of the Pops with them dressed as a Hell's Angel. I had to do some bopping with Charlie Grimmer (one of their drummers). Charlie was dressed in a ballet tutu. Wow!! What a day!

Don still had faith in us but he didn't know how to promote us. Warner Reprise were not interested in any other recordings from us. Don had to try to find a company who wanted us but most of his Company's energies were being poured into Wizzard and the new up and coming band,

ELO. We were sort of liked but lost (a kind of limbo) I had not come across this before. We were dressed up with nowhere to go and our album had stopped selling.

Chapter
$eleven$

SHAKESPEARE AND THE FROG

Don Arden offered us a tour with Wizzard. We would open their show for half an hour while Roy put his make-up on. I don't blame Don. He couldn't think of anything else to do with us. A Wizzard audience could never accept our kind of music. We would only be newspaper packing in the huge show case that contained Roy Wood. I knew right away that we were dying. We had become poor relations. For the first time in my career I felt talentless. It is at crossroads such as these that strength and courage is drawn from friendship. I need not have worried. The boys responded to this episode with their usual flair and humour, lifting me above my grey thoughts. 'Hold tight Frog; we are still with you!' Thanks H.

We threw ourselves into the tour and thoroughly enjoyed every moment. We had all grown up in the same streets as the Wizzard band so it was easy for us to get along.

I think it's true to say that the Wizzard audience found us instantly forgettable, but at least the exercise gave us our first experience of working with huge PA systems.

The frightening presence of thousands of enthusiastic people I found mind-blowing and extremely exciting. Rising to the challenge has stood me in good stead, for right up until the present day I feel completely at ease to perform to any size of audience, in any size theatre. Opportunities form experience in this great industry and I have been fortunate to have worked with some of the biggest stars in the business. This has enabled me to witness and learn some of the finer points of performance.

An artist will always have his (or her) own unique personality but it is essential to know the language of entertaining. This language, linked to your own style, is vital. An audience will never understand inexperience and they will be totally unsympathetic to your effort. After all, it's always necessary to remember that they pay you. If you disappoint them they will only pay you once.

I have always remained conscious of the fact that the money we earn has already been earned by the sweat and back of someone else. If they give it to me in return for entertainment then we had better be good at it. We can only be as good as our experience and we pay for that with disappointment, hard work, heartbreak and time. Time is no less precious to the seekers of leisure. They too know disappointment, hard work and heartbreak. In our pursuit of perfection we must stay in tune with life. Surely all people's trials are exactly the same. I write songs but everyone who listens actually lives them. I find contact in their presence and I am completely mystified by their pleasure. People throw stardust at me and, foolishly, I try to catch it. I balance on unsteady moments of joy and try to exist on the toxic area of dreams.

The Wizzard tour ended and we were still ingredients in this cauldron of success. ELO were the next outfit to receive the Don Arden touch of Midas magic. They had already had a small chart entry which did not mean much. Don decided to tour them. We would be used once again as the support band. The shows were not as well attended as those on the Wizzard tour, but we have to remember that every Wizzard single had hit the number one spot on the charts. To my mind, at this time ELO were still trying to find their direction. It was plain to see that they were going to be big, but something was missing. I was instrumental in helping to provide that missing need by introducing Jeff Lynn to the immense talent of Lou Clark. His eventual involvement provided width and class to this already wonderful array of talented musicians.

It was strange the way this introduction took place. As most things do in this business, it was another kind of accidental fall of fortune. Good for Jeff, good for Louis, good for Don, and great for the world of rock music. The Electric Light Orchestra was finally complete. Let me explain this extraordinary turn of fate that put my dear friend Louis Clark on to a high platform, where his vast knowledge of music and his great creative talents could magic their way through the songs of one of the most successful bands that the world has ever seen.

For two years I had been writing a musical based on the life of William Shakespeare. It was something of a hobby of mine, as opposed to a serious attempt at theatre. I had written it in my spare time. The research for this project gave me many months of relaxation. A sort of pleasure, where my mind could escape from the speed and pressure of popular music. I had mentioned this to Don just in passing conversation and surprisingly he immediately expressed a great interest in the prospect of recording the music and introducing the story to the business. You can imagine I was both shocked and flattered, because I knew that when Don said something he rally meant it. I explained to him what sort of budget we would need to embark upon such a venture. We would need a full symphony orchestra, and forty singers. In addition to this there would have to be an orchestral arranger and musical director. Only the largest, most expensive recording studio would be able to provide the facility that such a massive undertaking would demand.

Don Arden never talks small. He just said to me 'Organise it. Employ whoever you need, and do it'. All things seem to have a pattern to me because the very next day after this instruction had been given to me, Louis Clark telephoned to ask if I would see his going-away concert. His four year course had been completed and he was ready to return to the industry. I witnessed Louis's concert, drank some beer, and talked over old times.

Louis was very keen to get to work on the Shakespeare project.

Not only did it give him the opportunity to get back to work in a big way, but the challenge of something so complex would enable him to use all of his fine attributes to their fullest extent. If I may be a little self-complimentary, perhaps I would tell you that he was very impressed with the book and the music I had composed. Praise indeed from such an outstanding musician, as he most certainly is.

You can imagine the amount of work involved for Louis to orchestrate two hours of songs and also write choral parts for forty singers. He had to be aware of vocal feel. The part of an actor will play has to keep its individual personality in song as well as in dialogue. This task has a great deal of composition, as well as orchestration, in order for the arranger to preserve the continuity of style necessary for the overall contribution of an actor's character. There would also be the time and energy-sapping composition of an overture, taken from the full complement of songs involved in the musical. A mammoth task but I knew Louis was up to it. Don Arden had suggested that I employ an already established orchestral arranger, but I convinced him of Lou Clark's potential. Don agreed to go along with my suggestion and because of Louis' later involvement with ELO I don't think he has ever regretted the decision.

We gave ourselves six months to prepare the whole thing, ready for our first visit to the studio. I booked the Music Centre in Wembley to do the recording. This studio is used to record most of the very famous film sound-tracks in world cinema. Studio One can accommodate up to three hundred musicians and singers. I booked the Mike Sammes

'Romany Way' Frog's current backing singers.

107

Singers to do all the vocals, with the exception of one character - an old pub-singing lady of less than virtuous standing. For this part I employed the lovely Rita Webb. I'll tell you about her later.

During the next six months the band and me were still performing in the universities. There was a kind of invisible discontent which had become our constant companion. Not a discontent in each other's presence, just a mist of feeling that, on reflection, was probably the movement of our dignity. The disappointments which (because of our ages) were becoming increasingly more difficult to bear. Individual horizons were showing themselves to us. How long can you run after something that kicks you off every time you catch it?

Our tears were beginning to flood our spirit. Our lives needed change. There is no well full of love enough that will fill the needs of a growing life. Hearts crack before they break and all around me I could see the searching eyes of boys who had become men. Sailors who had become afraid of the sea. Soldiers who were hurt and no one cared about their wounds.

Len Ablethorpe, my drummer and great friend, spoke quietly and told me that he was emigrating to Canada. His wife Barbara had her family already there. 'Good luck, Len. Please don't every change. I will always remember you. Please find in your life all of the dreams we together failed to reach. Reaching for them with you was unforgettable. I wouldn't change a day.'

H. Cain was restless and decided to take his wife and children on a tour of North Africa. He bought a caravan and drove away for a year. Somehow I knew we would work together again. We had been closer in all we did than most musicians ever experience. H. has a sixth sense to the needs of my music. He was the originator of our sound and I doubt if could have achieved anything without him. Have a safe journey old mate. I will look at every morning and compare it to our friendship.

Mick Hinks got married and settled (as we had) in Stratford upon

Avon. He started his own building company and as far as I know, he is still there. My original band with its form of music become echoes of distant laughter ringing and ringing. The memories and joyful deeds were now merely shadows. Only we will remember them. I shall not look for my friends in darkness for they were bright then, and they will always be bright. Their young years were sunlight. We gave our youth to each other and so shall we shine. Don't look for us in gloom. Four weary dreamers had played their final tune together.

Now, after fifteen years, I could come off the road. In our association we had learned many things. We had argued about the most trivial matters and stuck together through the most serious. A proper united human effort, blessed with mutual respect and genuine love.

My life from this point on was to take many crazy turns. I was like a flea who couldn't find a dog to catch. For the next six months I worked closely with Louis and together we had created a mammoth three hour (ready to be recorded) musical story. By this time Louis had moved his family back to Hockley Heath, a small village near to where I lived at Wooten Wawen.

The morning arrived. Our first day in Studio One. I picked Louis up at his home at 7 o'clock in the morning, and with a car boot full of manuscripts, instrument parts, choral parts, lyric sheets and a master score manuscript, we headed for London. We arrived at 9.30 am. The studio had been prepared. Our operator and engineer were ready. A steady stream of musicians and singers began to drift in. A seemingly endless multitude of players chattering and tuning up their instruments. I noticed among the string section that a book of porn was being passed

109

around. I heard one violinist say (in his Tory voice) 'This is a book on the Enigma Variations'. He was referring to a the classical piece composed by the great English composer, Elgar. The comparison to this and pornography gave rise to haughty chuckles among the generally upperclass string section, as opposed to the guttural guffaws with comments like 'look at the tits on that' from the brass and percussion section.

The studio was packed. The engineer was busy positioning everyone. Louis, myself and Mike Samme retired to the Bar Restaurant to discuss our plan of attack. As we talked I could see from the huge bar window the Wembley Arena. That place was going to play a great part in my life, but at that time I could have had no idea how or why. The musicians were set. Forty singers were poised - lyric sheets and manuscripts in their hands. Louis Clark on his conducting rostrum, our engineer Richard Goldblatt at the controls of the console, our tape operator had loaded the multitrack recording machine. I was in the Producer's chair and the red light was on. As Louis raised his baton, the silence was deafening. I knew at that moment that I was in at the deep end. If I were unable to swim now there wasn't a a soul in the world who could save me. I was looking at fifty thousand pounds worth of commitment and I was responsible for the lot. Due to the sheer size of this orchestra and choir it was bound to take a long time before all the individual contributions could weld together in one sympathetic harmony.

The problem for the singers was their phrasing of lines in order that their voices would seem to be acting in sound. The singers taking the lead parts would have to get into character. I could direct them to an extent as I had written the parts so I knew the mood of the various changes in the meaning of the lyric. Professionals respond magnificently to direction if the direction is given properly and not in a barrack square, bombastic self-opinionated, rigid, bullying way. None of us know everything but everyone knows something. When in the entertainment industry, take my tip and listen to them all, then you will learn much more than you've got to teach.

Louis had made a great job on the orchestration, and his conducting created a perfect example of the traditional musical. We were getting along just fine. An orchestra is split into sections and each section has its own leader. The orchestra has an overall leader (the lead violin) and he is under the direction of the Conductor arranger. The Conductor will try to convey the meanings of the writer to the whole conglomeration of musicians. The writer will then either smile or cry. I did a lot of smiling that first day. To write a musical takes only time, but to record one takes time and compromise. After all, when you marry technology to anything it's problematic. The temperament of electronics and the temperament of artists are both just as unpredictable and mystifying as each other. We had the best engineer we could have hoped for in Richard.

Panic and loss of valuable patience were not part of his make-up. He handled every technical and electronic hang up with the hand of a saint and I had an expert engineer and a superb music director. So I was producing in armour. Do you remember the importance of getting the right people around you when making your music?

It was obviously going to take us weeks to complete, but a good first day sets your confidence high. Our previous years working together had given Louis and myself an inner understanding of each other's style and preference. In music these chemistries are helpful because they open the doors of humour and make frustrations more easily laughed at.

The important thing for us was that we now knew we could complete what we had started. We got to our hotel in the early hours of the morning, sat down, had a few beers, and talked, sometimes about the musical, sometimes about the past. How about our futures? I had no doubt that Louis would succeed in our business. He simply had too much to offer to fail. He needed a break. The Shakespeare Musical provided him with his introduction to the big time. If the musical only ever achieves that then to my mind it was well worth writing.

On one of our days in the studio Jeff Lynn was working in the complex with his band. They all came into our studio to see what was going on. When Jeff saw the ssymphony orchestra at work with Louis conducting his eyes fell open. He knew Louis of course from the days when we were kids playing in Birmingham, but I think it shocked him to see how accomplished he had become.

I told Jeff that he should use full orchestra sounds on top of his electric orchestra, and employ Louis to arrange and conduct. The next day Jeff Lynn had Arthur Sharp ring me (Arthur is the ex-singer of the Nashville Teens and works for Don Arden in a liaison capacity). Would Louis be interested in arranging orchestra and conducting for the next ELO album? He was, he did, and the result is history. Louis received his first gold disc and his future was sound. Louis Clark doesn't owe Jeff Lynn, or me, anything. His natural talent is a compliment to anyone who is fortunate enough to work with him. Louis worked on all of the ELO albums after that and because of his success has arranged for Elton John, Bill Wyman and many other stars. His 'Hooked on Classics' records have sold millions of copies, making him a household name in many parts of the world.

We still had the musical to complete and it was well on the way to the stage when Don would pay us a visit. One thing about Don is he never looks over your shoulder while you are working. The construction of music doesn't interest him. He likes selling it.

We got to the point where we were ready for Rita Webb. She wanted to work on a mid-day. She told me she keeps falling to bleedin' sleep after that!! I went to Rita's home to pick her up. I had already been to meet her three weeks before to rehearse exactly what I wanted her to do. I spent a delightful day in her company. Rita and her husband Jeffie were wonderful hosts. To be with one of our country's top comedy actresses in her lovely home was a great thrill for me. How strange it is how little we ever know about people who are so familiar to us because of their appearance on our television screens or the cinema. How narrow the roles they play, and how small an insight we get into their vast talents. I remember Rita saying to me that she could never understand why they chose Anna Neagle to play Queen Victoria, as Rita could have acted that part easily, and she looked more like Queen Victoria than Anna Neagle did. Anyway, 'If there was a bucket of shit and a mop in the role they would send

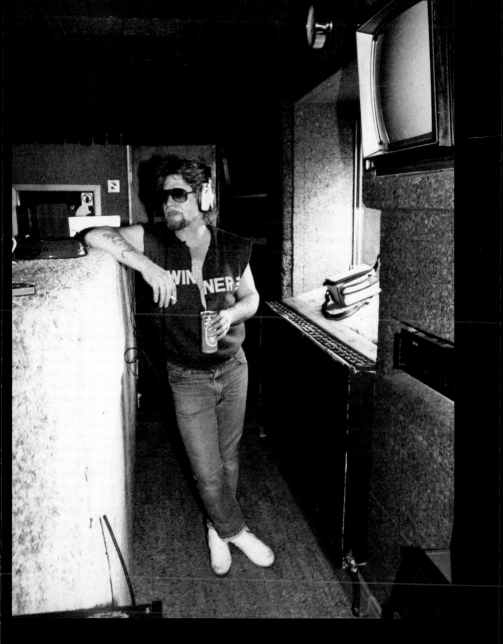

He Even Uses The Recording Console as A Bar.

Brownie & Froggie, Sense Prevails.

Froggie & Kenny Johnson in conversation at Lyme Park.

Brownie & Froggie

Frog at The Albert Hall.

Left to Right, get together Mick Hinks, Frog, Len Abelthorpe, H.Cain

Frog & Tad, with his neighbours, The Frank Tribe, the dear children

Frog with Polish Band (Country Roads)

H & Lynn decided it was time to get married, best man Froggie.

Frog with William Hunt Minders & Thomas Farnell.

God Bless Bill

'Titch' The keen Follower, Yea Man!

for me'. Lovely Rita.

Rita Webb wrote poetry and I was fortunate enough to hear her read it in the tranquility of her own home. She had the most beautiful and articulate speaking voice, full of richness, sadness, joy and caring. Her poem 'Cuddle While We Can', which she had dedicated to her husband, Jeffie, was quite the most moving piece of work I've ever heard. I could tell that their love for each other was total, as real and as big as the stars. Rita's stories of working with Arthur Haynes and Benny Hill were (as you can imagine) more than a little interesting.

This was the first time Rita had recorded with people like us and our way of working was completely alien to her but, bless her heart, she gave it all she had got. Simply magnificent!

Rita's arrival at the studio caused a complete shutdown. Everyone wanted to meet t1his lovely lady, who had been making us all laugh for so many years. I was talking to the lady in charge of the restaurant. She said they had been visited by Bing Crosby, Anthony Newley and Leonard Bernstein, but no one was more enthusiastially received than Rita. She handled the general euphoria with absolute grace and pleasurable warmth. It occurred to me as Rita was singing her part that I had done what everyone else had done in this business; I needed an old woman pub singer of ill repute so I sent for Rita Webb. Shame on me.

I told you earlier of the silence just before you record. Here we had a full symphony orchestra, Louis Clark on his rostrum, Rita Webb at her microphone and the red light was on. Louis whispered to Rita, 'I will cue you with my baton at your entry after the introduction has been made, so watch me closely'. 'All right darlin''. Louis tapped his baton on the rostrum edge. The orchestra responded. Their fifteen bar introduction was made. Louise beckoned for Rita to sing by pointing, giving her a bar of music to start singing. At that point dear Rita began to sing immediately, causing the whole orchestra to fall apart in magic mirth. Louis tried to explain to Rita that she should wait for four beats after his directional point. Rita's report was 'Well, you waved your bleedin' stick dain't ya'?' She did a superb job in the end and a great day passed by quickly, as all nice moments in life pass, leaving warm thoughts in the minds of all of us who enjoy the pleasure of human company. Rita and I became friends until she sadly died, leaving a public of laughing souls whose memories will surely always skip a little every time they hear the voice, and see the face of one of the great comedy actresses of our time. Rita once said to me, 'Froggie, let us not be ships that pass in the night'. They were the very last words she spoke to me. Rita, I will sail on your memory for always. Rest in peace.

The recording of the musical was finally complete. It had taken me two years to write and seven weeks to record. Don Arden, quite out of character, loved it. His enthusiasm for the work was extraordinary. Louis Clark was immediately put to work with the ELO. The second stage of his great career had begun.

Don Arden suggested to me that the dialogue for the actors' parts should be written by an established proper playwright, and I agreed. He fixed up a meeting with Terence Feeley. He had a great pedigree, having written all of the Avengers programmes and also a more highbrow programme series called 'The Prime Ministers'.

Dinner was set at the Hilton Hotel, Park Lane, London. I arrived at Don's house in Wimbledon at 6 o'clock in the evening. We got into Don's Rolls Royce and made our way to Terence Feeley's home to pick him up. Don put all of his gold on - I suppose to impress some people. He looked like a million dollars. I've never been a very dressy sort of bloke, and the crotch had split in my old black jeans. I spent most of the night trying to conceal my niagras! Terence had a beautiful trendy central London home, huge and very tastefully done out with expensive things, the likes of which I had never seen. He was dressed in what looked like a pin-striped morning suit, obviously very expensive and very proper for dining out in London. Next to these two wealthy people I looked like a bag of shit, but I had washed my white pumps in honour of the occasion. I arrived at the Hilton with two very important people. We were shown to our previously reserved table situated in a requested secluded corner. We ordered our various preferences. I remember that Don and Terence made a warm hearted jest of me having steak and chips. I think they were both shocked when I ordered escargot, French veal escalopes, garlic mushrooms and roasted spinach meat loaf. I might be a scruffy bugger but I know how to order grub! These people were posh and rich all right, but we were together to discuss business about a musical that I had written, so I wasn't out of place. I knew, and so did they, that I could match them in conversation about music.

We talked and measured our way through each other's different needs; fees, time, and suggestions of change were openly stated. Terence made a point about a line I had written in one of the songs. It was 'the beauty of children that came from our bodies'. He said he found that slightly obscene. I reminded him of his script for the movie called Percy. The story of a transplanted penis. He went strangely quiet. Three hours later we had discussed all of the finer points of the business and enjoyed our meal. It was now a matter of time for thought, having met each other could we work together? We ordered brandy and on its arrival the waiter bought a telephone - an urgent call for Don. It was a hysterical Lynsey de Paul. She had recently signed herself to Don's Company and the call was to inform him that the local children in her neighbourhood had posted dog shit through her letter box! Could he please call round as soon as possible? Terence asked why we didn't go round there now, he would love to meet Lynsey. Don agreed and off we went.

Our arrival was greeted by a very irate and tearful Lynsey de Paul. Don introduced Terence to her. I already knew her. She had been going around with Roy Wood at the time we had worked on the Wizzard tour. She attended most of the concerts and I have always found her a most agreeable young lady indeed. Here we were then, a top record company mogul, a screen script writer of the highest acclaim, a beautiful girl singing star, and me. Who do you think had to clean the dog shit up? You got it in one. I had started the evening in a Rolls Royce, dined on escargot at the London Hilton, discussed the possibilities of a filmed musical I had written, and ended up shovelling shit. That's Showbiz.

Terence Feeley didn't work on the musical. He informed the

office of his reluctance, claiming that the musical was in too much of an advanced stage for him to have the freedom of his own expression. That was his story and he stuck to it. I eventually did the script myself. The musical was taken to the States by Don Arden and he sold it to ATV Music in Los Angeles. It was filmed for television as a four hour blockbuster TV spectacular. One day no doubt I will open the TV Times and see it advertised. Until then my musical will lie in its can among hundreds of other films waiting for a future programme planner to find it worthy of a showing.

I learned many things from the making of Shakespeare. The discipline and time application of daily writing; production in studio orchestral recording; the handling of temperament in times of frustration. I learned how to appreciate the very inner, and sometimes invisible, unconscious efforts of contribution in others. How to release from them that little bit of extra from their musical talent - sometimes an extra they themselves could not see.

The joy of working with true professional musicians is something I find almost impossible to describe. They have so many different levels of creativity. These levels, coupled to their sometimes uncanny perception of lyric meaning, is a wonderful asset to any songwriter. A song is the idea and the canvas of a picture. The musicians are the colours and the painters - such painters I know. The musical is done. Let me not rest on that. Yesterday is yesterday and tomorrow is tomorrow.

Beardless Frog with George Hamilton IV.

Chapter twelve

INSIDE OUT AND UPSIDE DOWN

By this time ELO had become huge, selling millions upon millions of albums. They had also become one of the echalants of touring bands, grossing millions of dollars a show.

It was the time for Don Arden to form Jet Records and move to the States. He bought an office block in Los Angeles, and Howard Hughes' old mansion in Beverley Hills. He kept his two houses in Wimbledon and moved to America. Wizzard had disbanded and Lynsey de Paul had brought a law suit against Don for mismanagement. I was with Don when he received the writ. He simply made a paper airplane of it and muttered 'Silly cow!'.

I asked Don to release me from my Contract but he refused and told me that soon he would send for me to go to America to join Jet Records. Because of my own foolishness and lack of business acumen I was unknowingly falling into financial trouble. I had a business manager at the time but, unfortunately, he was a little dishonest. I won't mention his name because is now dead. He died in an accident on board a cross-channel ferry. For me to drag up blame and throw vengeance at his memory would not be fair on the lives of his wife and children. So he is gone now. He took with him any harsh thoughts I might have held and I forgive him. My band had gone, my record company had moved its head office to the States and

I found myself with nothing to do. Almost overnight I lost my lovely home, my two Range Rovers and Daimler Sovereign. I had unknowingly incurred thousands of pounds worth of debt through my Manager's misuse of my Company's credit cards. As people do, everyone around me ran like rats. My two road managers went to America and joined the ELO. My cheque payments from my song writing had been intercepted for months and extortionately endorsed with my forged signature. I received a solicitor's letter from the youngest of my road managers, informing me that he was going to sue me because he felt I should be responsible for paying his tax. This was the man that I had employed for six years, and when he moved into a home with his girlfriend I had his complete home carpeted as a present. I also had bought him a Willis jeep for his birthday. I replied to his solicitors that I would be prepared to go to Court and I would be informing the proceedings of their Client's dishonest claim for Social benefit whilst I was paying him. I didn't hear any more from them.

Louis was in America, H. was in Africa and Len was in Canada. I was, for the first time in my professional life, completely alone and in debt up to my neck. Everything I owned had to go to my creditors and I found myself homeless. I have to say that I felt a great deal of hatred for the people who had abused my trust and I couldn't think of one person who would help me. It soon got around the music business that I had fallen and I am bound to say there were many companies who would have signed me up, but Don wouldn't release me. So I was sunk. I found out later that he couldn't release me because he had sold my next five unrecorded albums to major companies and was obligated to honour his deal. I suppose he hoped I would fade away into oblivion (this would have given him an 'out' of that obligation) he didn't know me very well. I refused to fade away. Everyday I am just a day old. I'm as new as the morning. I wasn't born rich so I knew how to live in the street, and I still do.

Edward Fewtrell is a nightclub owner in Birmingham and was the first man to open a late-night drinking place in Birmingham We had become great friends from the early Sixties. He knew me as well as anyone. He knew he couldn't offer me financial help because I wouldn't have accepted it, but very kindly he offered to allow me to stay in one of his run down Victorian properties, for no rent. I said I would. The house was three storeys high and completely empty. I hadn't any furniture but a six by three piece of sponge from the market, and two blankets which, other than the clothes I stood up in, became my only possessions. To keep body and soul together I did some singing in local rock bands for beer and bread. If I had a few bob spare I would buy myself some luxuries - one week I was able to buy myself a camping stove and a saucepan.

I had made up my mind to get through this period alone because it was my own doing that had put me there. I hadn't taken care of business, and this was the result. I had one photograph of my old band left. I pinned it to the wall and their faces and memory inspired me to keep writing. I wrote song after song on the back of old wallpaper, which I had found in the attic. If anything could save me it had to be my songs. They became my future and my constant companions. I was in the company of spiders, but at that time I preferred them to people. I lived with the blue light of the most Spartan existence, but somehow I felt an inner strength that came from my past. The fleeting colours of disarrangement comforted me because I hadn't lost the will to try to win. I was going to get out of this, and I knew it.

Ozzy Osbourne came to visit me one day and he stayed for two nights. He bought a stack of beer and we stayed awake for twenty-four hours. He reminded me of the time that he slashed the tyres of my Daimler, just so I would have to stay at his home overnight and get drunk with him. He invited me back to his home in the country just to relax for a week. I consented. To be in an environment of opulence and peace for a short time helped me a great deal. Thanks Oz!!

H. Cain had been home for about six months but he couldn't find me, until one day my door clanged and echoed through my world. 'Hello Frog. How are you doing?' To see my great friend and his wife was my first feeling of warmth since I had entered those bleak days. 'We've bought you a piece of carpet. We heard you live on the boards these days!' He invited me to come and stay with his family, but he knew I couldn't accept. He told me he was playing for a lot of different bands, and doing some studio session work. His fine guitar playing has always been in great demand and always will be. When he left my rooms (I hope you don't mind) I wept for the first time, not from self-pity, but because I had just been in the company of a true friend. His visit had been the first light I had seen for almost two years. It is a light I have followed ever since.

I had a sudden urge to ring Don Arden in America. If there was a connection for me in the business then he was it. Like it or not, I was going to try humble pie. Anyway in the past two years I had eaten worse. Eddie Fewtrell let me use a phone at one of his clubs, and to my astonishment Don was available. 'Where have you been Raymond? I've been trying to reach you for months. I want you to come to America and make an album for me'. 'Can I bring H. Cain with me Don?' 'Sure, get your arse over here. I'll send you your air tickets and some expenses'. Inside out and upside down? Not for me.

H. Cain fancied going to the States like most people in this business. America to a musician has a sort of call to Mecca obsession about it. Opportunities to go there to perform or to make an album are rare indeed. So this, for us, was a most fortunate prospect, with the added ingredient of complete surprise. The music business is a dreadful blow dealer, but also a first class surgeon for the sometimes incurable disease of failure. The medicine in this case not discovered by Louis Pasteur, but by the test tube experimentations on rock music delved in by Don Arden.

We were to fly from Heathrow Airport direct to Los Angeles. A car would be waiting to take us to our hotel. Other instructions as what came next - my dears: we had none! WE were like children chasing the circus, hoping we would get home before we got lost. The call of the razzamatazz had us walking. The distant sounds of painted clowns, tearful underneath their cheap satin clothes, the smell of performing animals all around. Everybody should be somewhere else. The beast and the man all live amid the strangeness in this artificial jungle of lights. We are all born in more simple places than t hose in which we sometimes find ourselves. All of us walk to where we are and we can all return home if we choose, can't we? I shut the door of my borrowed home and left for the United

States of America. This hermit crab needed a new shell, try and make sure you don't get eaten while you're looking this time.

Chapter thirteen

MICKEY MOUSE, MEMPHIS AND ME

H. Cain, Froggie and a bottle of vodka arrived at Heathrow Airport. It was a joy for me to be travelling with my old mate again. One thousand dollars, two return tickets to LA courtesy of the London office, and a bunch of songs - my companions which seemed to accompany me everywhere. Words on paper held in pockets, travelling for free. One pocket full of dollars and one full of tunes. You can't sing a dollar and you can't spend a song. Both are light to carry and both can break your heart. We four together were chasing a new start. I hope we find it.

Sixteen hours later we arrived in Los Angeles. All of those years had gone by and two men out of four finally made it to America in the name of our music. I often wonder at the different levels of various people's ambitions. It's true that a certain achievement will satisfy one person, while another will see that sole achievement as failure, or merely a step towards their ultimate gain. I don't think that any of us know exactly where we are going or how far we want to reach. I believe that some of us just run out of steam and decide to settle for that. It is easy to compare ambition with greed, but surely it's folly to think that the ambitious are cursed with avarice. In my experience it has been the lazy, parasitic twisters that have shown greed and contempt to me. Ambition seems to die in them at the very mention of hard work. Their aim as far as I can see is to steal and abuse your trust. Invade your confidence then slander your competence while they are spending your money. At the age of fourteen I was working in scrap yards in Birmingham. Car breaking, weighing in scrap non-ferrous metals, sorting sacks and ammunition boxes. I came to know all types of people, the avaricious I have just mentioned, were all over the place. There are also the non-ambitious who, because of their nature, are happy to tag along odd-jobbing it, just getting through their day. Because of the natural indifference to forward movement it would seem that opportunities are wasted on them. Not so. To my mind they are less demanding on everyday things. Opportunities to them are a day's work for a day's pay, and the ambitious need them as much as they need their ambition. Shame on those who expect everyone to be a genius. A greedy man will earn nothing, give nothing and criticise all around him in order to hide his ill-gotten plunder.

I have grown up with young boys who, like me, worked in the lower order of business called the scrap metal trade. This daily bread work holds some of the finest despicable people I've ever known! It has spawned great businessmen, and men who are doing twenty years in the nick! I've loved them all. Some of my non-show business friends are people who have worked with me all those years ago. I still meet and enjoy their company now, as I did then. Brian Jubilee worked with me breaking cars when we were both teenagers. It's strange how our different ambitions took us into different worlds of business. He has become the owner of the leading car components suppliers in Europe, Jubilee Spares and Jubilee International, and I travel the world making music. We both started off breaking old cars with sledgehammers and hacksaws. We still meet every two months or so and spend a day together. We quote philosophical lines to each other from recent books we have read. We never talk of music or cars. Mentions of the future and the past are missing in our meetings. Each of us knows how hard the other can work and both of us have, on many occasions, worked for nothing. Our conversations are lightly political and have a relaxing, informing nature. We are two former grease monkeys who haven't forgotten the dirt we have washed from our bodies at a sink which belonged to somebody else. They let us use the sink, they sold us the soap but, in fairness, they always let us keep the dirt. Ambition is a great industrial cleaner and my ambition had brought me to America. I will wash a little more music from my soul and hope it doesn't disappear down a plughole like the grime of my youth - gone forever.

It was almost exactly the same time on the next day as we had left London the day before. Therefore it had taken us sixteen hours to travel while time had moved a full 24 hours. This phenomenon is supposed to give you what is called jet lag. H. Cain didn't feel it and I was too drunk to notice that the plane had even left the ground in the first place! Immigration clearance in America seems relaxed and friendly when you compare it with other countries. I suppose it's because the Americans feel safer and more confident in their environment than most other lands. Every American I have ever had to pleasure to meet appears to love the British people. I believe there is a definite bond between us and the strength of it, I'm sure will never be broken.

A driver holding a card with Jet Records written across it, stood waiting in the Exit Hall. We made ourselves known to him and after 'Hi! Welcome to America!' he drove us to our hotel, situated in Hollywood. The driver made sure we were settled in, and left. We never saw him again. We took a nightcap and turned in. A bed in Hollywood, California, has no special appeal. It might just as well be a bed in Aston, Birmingham, when you're knackered.

The bedside phone rang at noon the next day. We had slept for twelve hours. H. told me that he had had a restless night and found it difficult to relax because of the heat and excitement. After all, we were in Hollywood, so two kids from Brum were entitled to feel a little high. It was Don Arden on the phone. Had we got everything we needed? Did we like the hotel? Were we happy? Would we like a car for a few days? We could take three days to look around and generally enjoy ourselves before he needed us to meet people. Don sent a red Ford Mustang for us to ride about in, and H. drove us everywhere. Our hotel was beautiful, set in the Hollywood Hills, with swimming pools, bars and restaurants. We loved it.

In the evenings we sat drinking and working on the arrangements to our songs. On the fourth day Butch Parker came to the hotel. He introduced himself to us, informing us that Don Arden had employed him to produce our album. Butch Parker had been a keyboard player for Elvis Presley's concert orchestra, but had now progressed to a freelance producer, mostly working under the ATV Music of America Company banner. My music, now being published by ATV made Butch Parker their obvious choice to produce our work. In America, as you can imagine, the budget to make an album is vast, and when the two companies paying are ATV and Jet Records, money really is no object. Butch Parker had a free hand to employ whoever he wanted to record where he wanted, and to take as long as he needed. Butch decided to record the album at the Midnight Hour studio in Memphis. For the musicians he employed his mates, the Isaac Hayes Band. This band of players holds some of the greatest musicians in the history of music, since the first cavemen banged a stick on a hollow log. All people who have taken pleasure from their magnificent music will know how difficult it could be to gather them together in order to make an album with an unknown Englishman. I think it's proper that I should name them to you, so that you might see how very wonderful this business is, simply because of the artistes that dwell within it. First of all there was Steve Cropper - Midnight Hour Studio belongs to him. Steve played guitar for Otis Redding, and is a guitar player of immense talent. He has played on hundreds of works including Atlantic Crossing - Rod Stewart's legendary album, co-written Sittin' on a Dock on the Bay. I would need another book to tell you of his achievements. Anyway he was one of our guitar players. Bird Burton was another guitar player booked for the sessions. He played for the Rhythm Aces, a great country rock band. Donald 'Duck' Dunn was our bass player, another of Otis Redding's group. Willy Hall, drums. These four musicians were the band who played in the magnificent film, The Blues Brothers. In addition to these Butch also booked James Brown to play organ, Lester Snell to play piano and Michael Toles to play additional guitar. The Memphis Horns would provide the brass. The studio was booked for our first session six weeks from the day we arrived in Hollywood, so we had six weeks to spend in the company of Butch Parker, going over our songs and discussing the arrangements. He invited H. and myself to spend the weeks at his home with his family. He said that it might be nicer for us to stay in a family atmosphere instead of a hotel for that length of time. His wife Linda and their twelve year old daughter, Lee

Anne, made us very welcome in their lovely home. Like every other Hollywood home, it was set in the hills, with a swimming-pool and sprinkler system which could provide their own rain. California is as beautiful as you can ever imagine, and we now had six weeks to enjoy and explore everything we had only seen in the movies. We moved into Butch's house and we couldn't have felt more at home. One of his cars was at our disposal any time we wanted to get out on our own. One day we decided to take a drive down the LA freeway into Hollywood. When we got into town H. suggested we go the pictures. Only a kid from Aston could be in Hollywood and think of doing that! We saw a film called Mandingo, had popcorn and ice-cream. Very nice too!

Don Arden rang the house one morning and invited us to lunch with him at the Beverley Wiltshire Hotel, the most expensive and exclusive hotel in the world. Butch Parker, H. Cain and Froggie arrived at the front entrance of the Beverley Wiltshire. Two enormous marble pillars formed the entrance and a red carpet ran the full length of the walkway right to the car doors.

I hasten to add that this carpet was not there to greet us especially. It is just considered that anyone who crosses that hallowed marble step is a very important person indeed. So me and H. were going to be VIPs for a couple of hours. H. doesn't like a lot of pomp but, like me, I think he was enjoying this little excursion into the world of the super rich. One porter drove Butch's car off to the parking area and other porter escorted us to the dining gardens. The sheer opulence of this setting for repast is almost undescribable. The dining tables are set on individual raised balconies amid thousands of tropical hanging plants, orchids, palm trees, waterfalls, cabanas, sun shades and remarkable delicate colours dancing in the Californian sun. The people were all seemingly blessed with beauty. All were bronzed and superbly dressed, decorated ladies like pictures painted by an artist who used a gold ingot as his brush.

Don and his wife, Hope, were already sitting at their secluded table. Don absolutely fitted in amid this fairytale setting. Indeed, if he had sat at Don Arden's table, Cary Grant would have looked like a pauper. Our place settings were very tastefully done with silverware, orchids and a fresh fruit display as a centre-piece. Don had a trolley of telephones next to his seat, always at work, sometimes at play, never dull and forever directing his, and your day. We sat and small talked for a while. We exchanged greetings and complimented our professional involvement. Don never asks what you are going to do, just where you will be doing it, when you will be doing it, and how much will it cost. The waiter came to take our orders and I ordered Pacific Lobster with Chef's Salad. H. Cain ordered omelette and chips and a coke. Why not? Don asked for three bottles of champagne and asked that the dust be left on the bottles. Dust on a man is frowned upon, but dust on a bottle of Don Perignon is a mantle of wealth. It's difficult to imagine what God must think of all this.

In the next six weeks we did many things. A VIP tour around Universal Studios as special guests of Tony Curtis, who at that time was Don's neighbour. We had a very interesting look into the magical world of movie making to see the actual house used in the film Psycho, and to watch how the Red Sea parted in the Ten Commandments, was absolutely stunning. They keep every prop from every film that has ever been made there. I remember looking at the cigarette end stubbed out in an ashtray - exactly how Humphrey Bogart had left it in the film Casablanca, and thinking it seems that in Hollywood they only throw people away. The place on the river where every Wagon Train episode featured its weekly crossing is situated two hundred yard downstream from where the river steamer used in the epic musical, Showboat, is moored. It stands like a great still ghost awaiting a script and paint, so that it can be once again released from its slumber. Across the way stands a huge Vietnamese village, mud huts, dirt roads and at the press of a computer button they can be transformed into absolute mayhem by the release of millions of gallons of water in the form of a flash flood. Gale force winds bend real palm trees to a 45 degree angle. Torrential monsoon rains begin from nowhere and in a matter of minutes the Californian sun is shining once again - amazing! If the Americans can create this for pretence, what on earth could they create for real? Frightening!!

We did have plenty of professional things to do in these six weeks. There were press receptions at Jet Records and at ATV music offices. We were asked to attending publishing awards' dinners in order to become acquainted with the high Hollywood set. I knew a lot of the writers there already - Ray Stevens and Neil Sedaka were just two I had known from functions in London. They were both of them somewhat surprised to see old Froggie amongst the dancing temporary dreamers of the entertainment industry. H. Cain and Froggie dressed in tuxedo junction hire wear - and loving every minute of it. We got stuck into the grub, drank plenty of cold beer, but our behaviour was impeccable. A long way from a piece of sponge in a room in a low down house, but that's where me and my songs had come from. Shame on me should I ever forget that.

We dined at the legendary Brown Derby restaurant where every film star we've ever heard about has their own tables. The illustrious stars of our grandparents' youth still walk as spectators through the bright modern fixtures of today. Their autographed caricature portraits adorn the walls. Walls, if they could speak, would probably tell you as many lies as their publicists. But then, who really wants to know anything ordinary about people who entertain us.

A full day at Disneyland with Butch, his wife, daughter and H. was simply a great joy. H. is one of those people, who, much to the delight of Lee Anne, will have a go on every mechanical thrower-upper, twister-rounder, gut-churning, fear provoking ride that has ever been invented. Whilst I could only cope with a gentle spin in Alice in Wonderland's tea-cups. Mind you, the overhead monorail train that led to the only bar situated in the Disney Hotel, saw plenty of me that day. It's funny how the monotrain seemed to get closer to the ground as the day moved on. It's a small world after all. Oh yes, it's a small world after all. Thank God for Mickey Mouse.

After several barbecues, wonderful fun, American hospitality, orange trees and Californian sun, it was time for us to leave for Memphis Tennessee. Goodbye my dears, I will see you again. Some of your are lost and I know it, but all of you will, one day, be found - that's for sure!!

Memphis from LA is about four hours in a plane but the time is strange in America. It was dark when we left and light when we arrived. So we left a night to join a day. A different heat, more humidity. Everyone is constantly wet. This was Elvis Presley country and this was his home town. The man I had lined up for six hours to see in his first film, Love Me Tender, when I was sixteen years old lived in this place. I had come here to make an album which was going to be produced by Elvis's ex-piano player. Life was becoming more interesting by the hour.

Memphis is the home of Holiday Inns and we were booked into the largest one there, overlooking the Mississippi River. Life in this town has a much slower place that LA, but it's just as interesting and we had a week to get acquainted with the place before we were due to record. A seven foot five inch black ex-basketball player, who didn't speak a word to us all the time we were there, was assigned to take care of our wellbeing.

He never left our side for seven weeks. He, a car and a driver named Tripp, were our own personal A to Z of Memphis. These two black fellows instructed us through Tripp's Southern drawl how not to get killed in memphis, the places where whites could go safely, and never to go anywhere without them. Tripp informed us of how an out of town white guy got filled full of lead by a copper-coloured girl whom he had mistaken for a prostitute. There are a lot of dollar killers here. Sometimes the bullets they use cost more than they steal - but they kill and steal anyway. 'So you boys think twice before you think beaver, yuh' hear?' We got the message all right. We had been on the road for years and anyway, the back streets of Birmingham ain't a Sunday morning on the river with Mummy and Daddy. So by now we had some idea how to keep out of trouble. These two wonderful black guys took us everwhere. Down to New Orleans, downtown Memphis, and even a forbidden drive into the ghetto. 'Don't you boys ever come down here without us. Even the alligators stay in the river down here'. Tripp took us for a drive along Elvis Presley Boulevard to see Gracelands. As we drove, Tripp told us of the love that the population, both black and white, of Memphis have for Elvis Presley. 'That guy could drive down here sideways at 100 mph and not even they Mayor would complain', exclaimed Tripp. Even though Elvis was away on tour a small band of disciples sat around the iron gates of his home. Some had travelled thousands of miles just to do that. Wow!!

Butch Parker had left us in the capable hands of our two black protectors while he sorted out a few last minute jobs and made ready for the sessions. We had thoroughly enjoyed our week and seen most of Memphis. We had the pleasure of meeting and talking to the ordinary black folk, and listening to the stories of their days. I could see music in every line and crooked finger of the old. The red shot marks in the whites of brown, sad eyes suggested pain that was hidden by their love of Jesus. Their promised land dwells in the voices of their senators. Rain falls in every corner of their existence. Their trust has been dulled by the clubs and bullets of their suffering. Their dignity shines through ragged clothes and their pride, though smitten and stained with the spit and venom of lesser men, is as young and perfect as the innocence of children. I have seen their hearts from the outside and I still hear the beat of their longing.

We walked through the doors of the Midnight Hour Studio on a Monday morning and we were greeted by the most frightening array of musicians that eyes might behold. Steve Cropper, Dick Dunn, James Brown, Willie Hall, Lester Snell, Bird Burton and Michael Toles. Now I play guitar like a cuckoo builds a nest - it just don't happen. I thought

'What the hell, even a good guitar player could look ordinary in this company'. So I picked up the alien creature and sang them my first song. All of the players sat around listening intently, some making notes and others whispering suggestions to each other. I wondered if they were say 'Shall we **** off?' H. Cain played along with me - short of wind but, bless him, he hung in. Well I finished the song and waited for the silence to be broken. Steve Cropper said 'That's a song that Neil Diamond wished he could write'. I'm sure he was being kind, but I felt home and dry. I could now work with these great musicians and enjoy it. H. settled among these players and became an addition to the guitar line up. My life has been filled with the delight of seeing and hearing musicians creating their own compositions of incidental complimentary musical lines that take their own form within a simple song that I have written. Their skill seems boundless to me and the unselfish application of their efforts always ensures the protection of the main melody line. They are in fact arranging within an arrangement, composing around something that has already been composed. In an orchestral piece every note for every instrument is written down. The musician will take that note from the manuscript and cast it in the air in the form of sound. A small electric band have no guide, only their own ears plus their total love for electric music.

These Memphis people had grown up together and because of that they had a god-given gift of understanding, not only for music but for their very line of life, so different from ours and yet exactly the same. Because of the natural growing of all things we are like trees; pines grow better among pines; oaks grow with oaks; starlings fly together and all sparrows sing the same song. Living things know where home is and all musicians know with whom they would rather play. We are a species of such strange feather that we are bound to display our roots and learning with music. Who better then to create this music with than those who have cried in the same streets as oneself? The Memphis musicians knew each other like the backs of their hands and it showed. Their minds were so open to sound that they were prepared to marry their talents with a stranger from England.

I knew as we got deeper into the recording that my songs were being 'Memphisised' but it didn't seem to matter. They stood up well to the 'southern black bash' of these outstanding players. As I watched them work they reminded me of the musicians from my home town. Although they played a totally different style than us, their humour and effort were much the same. When I think of the great people I have worked with my heart swells with joy and love.

Birmingham has always given birth to great musicians and at some time or other over the years most of them have played for me. When the band 'TheMove' finally changed, Trevor Burton came to play for me for twelve months. He never really enjoyed playing my music because his roots are firmly planted in the raw rock and blues tradition. He is a great rock musician with energy of staggering proportions. His own band, right up until today, has a great following and whenever I am in town I try to make an effort to see my old friends play. It is always a marvellous entertaining experience and Trevor Burton will live in the ears and souls of thousands of people long after his talent has been laid to rest. It's never wise to try to understand Trevor; just stand among the stone, sit on the night, turn your soul towards the storm and let your bones move on to Trevor Burton's electric world. Yeah Mon!

Roger Hill is one of the finest jazz guitar players in Europe. This boy from Birmingham has also played my music. Together with Trevor and H. Cain we played most of the universities and colleges in our country. Those were great days for me because to work with such different and individual stylists was a wonderful learning base for me to live on. Roger Hill eventually got to play for the amazing Stephan Grappelli. He also played many concerts with Fairport Convention and Chris Barber. A man of such worth is a joy to know. He played my simple song 'Roly' with the same incredible feel that he would display when playing the most complicated avant garde jazz piece - how unselfish and how complimentary. He is still one of my greatest friends. Because of both of our daily commitments we cannot see as much of each other as we used to. When we can get together however, the joining of free hours become most serious moments of unadulterated stone-blind drinkin' fun! One day I will say to God 'I met Roger Hill once and he played my songs' and God will know exactly who I mean.

There are musicians in our town who gave all of their efforts, time and youth to this business but never quite made it outside the area. Some of them still play with tremendous talent and great care. So you see there must be, I'm sure musicians in every town all over this world who for some unfortunate, sad reasons never quite found the way out of their time. They are the clouds that we all try to see through. They are the sun that shines on the fortunate. they are the tears that songs are made of; they are the time we all lived in. They ran with us, laughed with us, loved with us, hoped with us, cried with us, stripped naked their souls and failed. Still they are here, their dreams shattered and broken, yet every wheel of tomorrow's

young players will roll in their tracks. This road is made of a million broken hearts and a million broken dreams. This then could be another dream to be shattered, another heart to be broken, but a song that for now must be sung. Here in Memphis we are making an album and whoever made one thinking it would fail? Not me, or Don Arden, so play me some beautiful dreamy music my American friends and this Limey will sing you a song. H. Cain and I worked very hard day and night in order to complete this beast of notes and words. There were times in this effort when we were seen to be tired and restless. Even though we were strangers our hosts knew we needed some fun. We were invited to spend a day at Fats Domino's ranch. We accepted, of course, and a nicer day would be extremely hard to equal.

The great man himself was away on tour but his wife and children were at home. The southern hospitality of these wonderful people cannot be measured in words. We played in boats on a huge lake, rode horses in red, green and bluegrass fields. We ate ribs and burgers and drank beer beneath the scorching Tennessee sun. There were little black children following and chattering to us in untroubled joyfulness, protected by the wealth that their marvellous father's music had provided, a wealth he could never have known as a child. Because of his talent he was able to buy a piece of the country that had so cruelly whipped and humiliated so many of his black brothers and sisters in their struggle for freedom. As these children squealed with delight I could see coloured wings of strange butterflies dancing on the haze amid floating plant seeds, busy looking for a place to grow. In the distance I could see the great Mississippi river winding its way towards New Orleans. It seems to me that a river lives almost the same life as man. It begins small and pure, growing all the time. It can be kind and peaceful, allowing delicate things to play within its slumbering rage. It can turn at a whim, burst its banks, drown children, sink boats, flood; and in its wake leave destruction and weeping mothers. Without an apology it will steal away towards its own oblivion in the mighty ocean. Its seed will become clouds that rain upon the mountains. The rain will become the river, bearing its father's name. Following the same direction it too will be loved, sometimes kill and then die.

I watched the children shrieking with laughter at the sight of H. Cain trying to row a swamp boat and getting it all wrong. Triggered memories of my own childhood came flooding back. There were few trees and no lakes in Bordesley Green, Birmingham. There were horses though, but they all worked for the Co-op. They were stabled in a yard across the street from where we lived in Cherry Wood Road.

The war was in full flight and I can still remember a few of the terrifying air raids to this day. One night incendiary bombs were dropped in our street and almost every building was ablaze. We had to leave our shelter because of the heat and exploding gas. Our mom picked me up and held my sister Jean by the hand. We ran the full length of our street, which by now was blazing on both sides. The Co-op horses had escaped and were running blindly, in total panic. People were fighting the fires, children were desperate and crying. We made our way to the Diamond Screw Factory in the next street and mom banged on the factory shelter door. No one would open it so we sat in the well of the shelter steps and our mom covered us with her body. She was pregnant with my brother Jim, and because of our mother, we all survived the raid.

Shortly after that I fell ill with tuberculosis of the lungs and had to be hospitalised in the Yardley Sanatorium. I was four years old. It was 1944. I came out in 1947 and I saw my brother Jim for the first time. He was sitting in the gutter with a plaster over his eye and he was hitting the road with a stick. We made friends and began growing together. Two scruffy kids had made it, but our father had been killed.

The children were still laughing and H. was still trying to row the boat. I wrote a song that day called 'Here's to Butterflies'. The yellow pollen centres of the flowers and the green shiny leaves misted over as the heat waved a foggy sheen across my dream.

The day was over. I was happy and very slightly drunk.

We completed our album and decided to call it 'Memphis Moonshine'. We thanked our new American friends and said goodbye.

As we were flying back to Hollywood H. said that he would like to return home to his wife and kids.

We had to put some finishing touches to the album in Los Angeles but that didn't involve him. The next day I said goodbye to my pal and put him on a plan to London. I would follow on in about two weeks' time.

Butch Parker mixed the album at Hollywood Sound Studios and our job was done.

One of the tragic things of our industry is that, while an artiste's view remains simple, all around him major political changes are occurring to the Company he is involved with. The bigger the Company to whom you are signed, the more effective these changes can be on your future. For instance a recording company will be constantly dealing in the market place looking for outlets in different countries in order to sell their products more efficiently. At any one time an artiste's recording can be distributed by over a dozen different companies; one in Australia, one in Japan, one in Germany and so on. These are called 'area deals'. The area Company will obviously want the product that will take the minimum amount of promotion as promotion can cost hundreds of thousands of pounds. Sometimes millions of pounds are spent by these companies in order to obtain sole rights of distribution in their area. So it's plain to see that they will take their pick of a company's products in return for the vast amounts of front monies they are spending. If any artiste is unfortunate enough to be with a company that can boast many established bands then I am afraid he will not be part of the plans. His work will be shelved. It is better from the company's point of view to write the cost of your work off as a tax loss.

Beneath all these workings an artiste will be devastated and confused and according to the make of the man he will either disappear heartbroken or he will fight back. This was about to happen to me again as it had before with Bell Records.

The album 'Handle with Care' was shelved and now 'Memphis Moonshine' faced the same fate. They were both shelved for the same reason. Generally Don Arden wouldn't give a shit for the feelings of men because he looked at things in a purely business way. If anything stands in the way of his Company's progress then it must go down the tubes and that's that.

In my case, however, because of his genuine affection for me as an artiste, he was more sympathetic and decided to try something different.

Don broke the bad news to me concerning my album but he asked me if I would meet someone before I left for England. I felt bitterly disappointed but I am an optimist and said that I would.

I arrived once again at the Beverley Wiltshire Hotel. As always in Hollywood it was a beautiful morning. Don's son David Arden was there to meet me. David was more like us than his dad was, so instead of a formal lunch we decided to go to the Hotel pool and have a few drinks at the bar while we waited for this unknown person (to me) to arrive.

David gave me an outline of his father's plans for me. As our conversation developed I began to feel rather puzzled. Here I was with an album, hardly in its can, that was shelved and he was talking of me going to Nashville to make a Country album with the Jordannaires. Larry Butler would produce it and it would be made at Jack Clement's Studio.

I had heard of all these people but I couldn't see how I would fit in, or indeed if my songs could ever be recorded in this style. David had reminded me that I had once been turned down by Island Records for sounding too Country and perhaps it was worth a try,

As a songwriter I was, of course, familiar with Hank Williams' music and also that of Willie Nelson, Eddie Rabbit, Johnny Cash and others. They would be hard company to live with but David convinced me enough to give it a shot. If I was agreeable Don would pay the biggest British Country music promoter forty thousand pounds in order that this man's company could promote me on the British Country music scene.

First of all we had to make the album. At this point a very sharp character dressed in shorts and bathrobe, smoking a large, expensive cigar, approached us. David introduced us and we talked. The man told me of his arrangements for me to be taken to Nashville. I would be staying at the Hall of Fame Inn, one of the best hotels in Nashville. He chose this hotel because it was frequented by a lot of artistes and writers and would give me an opportunity to meet and get to know the scene.

He suggested that I write the songs for the album in Nashville itself. He felt that I might be inspired by the place. He assured me I would have all the time I needed to do so. He told me of his plan to introduce me to the British Country people at his huge festival held at Wembley every Easter. I asked him if these people, in his opinion, would like me. After all, I was completely unknown to them. 'Of course, they won't at first', he replied.

$\mathcal{C}$hapter fourteen

SOUTHERN FRIED FROG

The new project was going to take a few months to set up so I came back to England until I was sent for. H. Cain asked me to come and stay with his family until I was in a position to get myself a home. I really didn't fancy going back to that dirty room I had left, so I accepted gratefully.

I told H. about the fate of our Memphis album but, as always, my old friend made light of it and said 'We'll make a better one in Nashville'.

We got together with a few musicians and did a couple of gigs. Nothing serious - we were marking time, Although we were not earning much money all of our personal pressures had gone. We were still together and we had something to look forward to.

Eventually the call came. It was from Mervyn Conn. We had to meet him at Heathrow Airport the following week. He wanted us to travel with him to Los Angeles, spend two weeks at press calls and publishing dinners and then sign contracts, generally get to know each other and let Mervyn educate us on his rules and methods. They were fair enough. He asked us to conduct ourselves in a correct manner on stage and in public whilst we were under his banner. I understood that. H. Cain and myself have always been professionals. If we had not been we would never have gained the respect we have, right up until this day, in every area of our industry.

Mervyn asked us if we would like to call in at the American Country Festival in Tulsa, on our way to Nashville. If we wanted he could arrange for us to do a short appearance just to get the feel of a Country audience. We stayed with Mervyn at the Beverley Wiltshire. Although we have dined there we had never been guests. Post of what?!!!!

Two weeks later H. Cain, Mervyn and me caught a plane to Tulsa, Olklahoma. Our new career in Country music had begun. Mervyn did manage to secure us a guest spot - 15 minutes in the middle of the first night's show. We had the help of a drummer and base player from Leroy Van Dyke's band. We rehearsed for fifteen minutes, played 'Roly', 'Teach Me' and 'Always Goodbye'. Much to our surprise the American Country fans loved us and gave us a great welcome into the very close- knit world of Country.

I thought to myself (quite wrongly) that if the Americans liked us then the British fans were bound to. There was a very different world waiting for me in Britain and I was going to find out the hard way. Nothing in our business is easy and I have always loved a challenge. However strong our love is there will always be people who find it difficult to kiss us. What a pity.

Although I felt excitement at the prospect of this new direction there was, deep within me, a kind of sad foreboding. The feeling had me faltering like a wild animal at the door of a strange cage. I could not be sure there wouldn't be something in there that would eat me alive. I had never run away from anything in my life but, like all people, I have considered running many times. This business can bury you in fear. It's not only the waste of life in its waiting failure that scares you. It's the humiliation of your own self that can conquer your deepest spirit.

As a child I once left home for about an hour and I ran in a straight line so that I could find my way back to anxious arms. However straight or crooked you run in the entertainment business there will be no arms to welcome you home. The road you take is the road that you must stay on.

People will laugh at your failure or they will criticize your success. It is this sadness that makes clowns of us all. I will take the road to Nashville straight and true. I am only an innocent maker of songs trying to touch the hearts of people who don't really need me. So fall, my pretty ones, from this pen. Words we all speak - form yourselves, that I might find a place here.

We arrived in Nashville on a fine Tennessee morning with the usual rusty nail of hope pinning us to the slippery wall of the music industry. All of us musicians must be barmy really. Because we are never aware of the snapping jaws of thieves constantly trying to mould our talents into their income. We have to be oblivious to them otherwise we would deny our hearts the freedom to create music and then there would be nothing for them to snap about.

There are a lot of snapping thieves about in our business. They hide in dark corners waiting for an opportunity to get involved. They all have a little business acumen which they have generally developed in another industry. At first it's the glamour and the 'little Hitler' power they love to feel by gathering around them a bunch of skint musicians. Offering them sound, proper management, informing them with sweeping statements of ill-informed armchair philosophy of what the poor fools have been doing wrong for years. These people always fail to grasp the fact that these years of so-called foolishness are spent learning our trade and taking the risk which every entertainer has to experience in order to gain movement and audience.

You will never find the thieves in the early days. It takes too much guts and commitment for them to get involved. They don't like going without and neither do we. The difference between us is that we know that most times we have to. But at least we have courage and love enough to go without together.

The first thing they do is to take over the finances and negotiations. They know absolutely sod all about the entertainment industry so their negotiations always end in conflict, argument and failure. Bridge-burning goes on at an alarming rate. These are bridges which these people never helped to build and they are bridges which they will never have to cross. Consequently they smash willy nilly at everybody who doesn't agree with them. When these 'rag and bone man' antics fail the thief will put into operation Plan B. This is to grab as much money as he can and run.

First of all he will retrieve from the band's earnings any money he has contributed. He will usually call this move 'taking mine out'. His next move is to take everybody else's out also. This plan can take up to twelve months to achieve. He will put forward to the band a proposition that they would work every possible day at a killing pace so that enough money can be accumulated in order to do finer, more rewarding work, so that the band will feel dignity and security. This is called 'Promise Land'. A massive amount of dates are put together. These dates will provide the thief a platform from which he will sell the band's merchandise - usually albums, tapes, t-shirts, jumpers and anything else he can think of to sell.

The money from road merchandise is impossible to trace and the thief will be aided and abetted by someone close to him so that no one else can possibly see what is going on. Some of the dates will be cash paid fees and others legitimate, with VAT invoices given. There will only ever be enough money in the band's business account to fold it up. The business account is a smoke-screen for theft. What the thief calls 'black money' (proceeds from the merchandise and cash fees) will be salted away, usually at someone else's home - never his own, ready for his final move. The thief's double-cross has to be (for the sake of his image) a carefully manufactured public argument. He will criticise and provoke you with astonishing contempt so that you bite at just the right time. The thief will know that you will be completely exhausted from the amount of work you have done and he will know exactly the things to say that will provoke a tired man. The public argument, having took place, allows the thief to display a great performance of wounded innocence, the victim of immense ingratitude. His exit is final, his image is intact and the injustice paid to the band is unbelievable. He will outwardly look impoverished for a while but gradually he will start to recover - not too quickly. When the sweat of innocent musicians has dried from this money he will start to spend, and the band of players will play on.

The Americans have a saying in our business. It is 'Never give a sucker an even break and never trust your brother'. A hard philosophy you might think, but perhaps they know something that we don't.

If the thief is your brother he will even have the unspeakable gall to sit in the same room and breathe the same air as your mother. The weight of the despicable deed on his conscience will not bother him one bit. Even while the dung-heap of lies dwells in his twisted soul he will show the same contempt for her by stupidly thinking that he has also succeeded in fooling her and the rest of your family.

Something as tragic as this is not typical of the music industry and indeed not typical of most people that you meet in ordinary life. But it does happen. You see the trouble with someone like me is that I am a victim of my own refusal to give up. I have spent so many years in this business that I was bound to gather a certain amount of fans who remained loyal through thick and thin. There has never been enough of them to make me a real success, so that my manager, my players and indeed myself, could feel financially secure, among our (by the industry's standards) quite limited achievements. If we were only one person then our wonderful fans would make someone like me very comfortable indeed. We have, however, always been five of six people, all of whom work just as hard as each other. I have never felt myself to be more deserving of things than my fellow players for without them I have nothing. No fans, no day, no night, and no one to play my songs.

A non-professional, arrogant manager will consider the moral obligation to care for the needs of everyone involved to be a stupid waste of money and he will train his mind to resent musicians, thinking them unworthy of their weekly wage. This will induce him to steal in the manner I have explained. He will take everything and leave you with the sound of his contempt and scoffing mockery in your ears. His pockets will be full of pound notes earned by the music that simply bounced off him. Songs that flew through the air ricocheting off his cruel thick skin, will once again enter the ears of the fans who love us still, making us (unworthy fools) richer by far.

Mervyn Conn, H. Cain and me were met by Mervyn's limousine and taken to the Hall of Fame Hotel on the corner of Music City Row. Our superb room had a view of the Nashville skyline. These moments are unforgettable to a maker of music. After all, here we were in the Country music capital of the world with a countless number of miles, years, past moments of joy, heartbreak and lost friends still accompanying our every move.

This orchestra of ghosts still follows me and waits for the song I might compose, that their years of tuning up might be worthwhile.

A quick shower, change of clothes, a swift drink in the hotel bar and away we went, exploring the streets of Nashville. Music City simply throbs with atmosphere and every brick in every building echoes with the distant sound of long-gone and living legends. Humble beginnings, poor circumstances, mountain folk, cotton pickers and little girls in gingham dresses have rode mules, walked flew, driven, some crawled on hands and knees, boozed, drugged and lonely, their bones whipped bare with the lash of ridicule, stole precious time from their loved ones to come here driven by something that only God can see. Some of these magnificent, ragged, homeless walkers wrote songs of such greatness that the whole world stood and applauded. I came here in the hope that I might do the same.

Nashville is full of famous places and almost every store or bar had a name I had heard of. I was going to be here for six months at the very least so I felt no need to go 'hell bent head down full pelt' at every street sign. I was here to write songs and so it seemed important to me that I should get to know this city from inside its own skin.

At this time I didn't know a single soul in Country music, either in Britain or America. Mervyn Conn is not the kind of man to introduce you around. He just leaves you to it. I have always admired him for that because I feel he shows a great respect for a man's individuality. He is always watching but he leaves you to fire your own bullets.

Quite naturally I began to frequent the places where live music was being played and in Nashville that is not difficult as almost every lounge and club in town has something going on day and night.

Two or three weeks passed by and, after visiting every club and bar in Nashville, my pal and me had begun to make friends. Quite naturally, they were musicians - no one famous but great players just the same. Invitations to their private homes gave us a chance to sample that world-renowned southern hospitality. Fried chicken, home made Martha White biscuits, honey smoked ham, hickory baked bread, gravy and all. Simply wonderful people with hearts (like the song says) as big as all out doors.

The telephone rang at the Hall of Fame Inn and reception informed me that a Mr Larry Butler wished to speak with me. My moment of truth had arrived. Larry Butler was one of the most important record producers in our industry at that time. He had been responsible for many hit records. Among them were 'Blanket on the Ground' by Billy Jo Spears and 'Lucille' by Kenny Rogers. Larry was also making records for the legendary Johnny Cash. I was about to talk to someone who was very important indeed. My whole career and final chance to become good in this industry hung on the desperate threads of my past experience. Between Larry Butler and my songs there lay in wait the great vulture of failure. Either it or I had to go hungry. The outcome of this duel depended on the professional relationship that may or may not have formed between myself, my songs and Larry Butler, a man I had never met in my entire life. It is almost impossible for me to explain the dreadful pressure that moments like these can put you under. It was not as if I had just been discovered by someone who was going to show me what to do, someone to nurse me through moments of indecision and fear. I was expected to be good and in the company of world-famous people that expectation can be very daunting indeed. I knew, because of my experience of past recording, that the mechanics were the same the world over. This however, for me, was not only a different recording technique it was also a totally new concept and style of music. I felt hopelessly inadequate and found myself digging deep within my soul in the hope that I might find the inspiration and courage to stand side by side with strangers.

'Hello Larry'! 'Hi Froggy, how are you finding our little town?' 'Fine thanks. I am looking forward to meeting you'. 'Well, that is going to be tomorrow, I will be in town about mid-day. I want to hear some of these songs you write. I have been hearing all about you from your old friend Roger Cook. He lives in Nashville now you know'. I felt a great feeling of joy. I had known Roger Cook since his days with Blue Mink This magnificent song writer had composed many hit songs in his life. Amongst them was the classic 'Coke' theme, 'I'd like to teach the world to sing'. I knew that he would have said some complimentary things about me and I felt a little less concerned now that I had a friend from the old days in Nashville. Larry gave me his Nashville number and said 'I'll see you soon Froggy, and if you get lonely you give me a call. Ya Hear? Bye now'.

I wrote a song that day called 'Give me a Call' and it was the first song I played to Larry when we met. He loved it. Larry booked a room at our hotel. He told me that he was mixing a Billy Jo Spears record called '57 Chevrolet' in the same studio were we would be making our album. His invitation for me and H. Cain to sit in on one evening was very welcome because it gave us a chance to see the studio and to meet Billy Jo Spears. I didn't know it then but BJ and me were to become great friends. She is truly one of the nicest people I have every known. A great singer and an immensely fine artiste of stunning professionalism and the best poker player since Maverick!

H. Cain informed me that in about ten days time he would have to return home. Unlike me, he had pressing family concerns which demanded his presence there. We, in our industry, have to understand each other's personal commitments. It is absolutely vital that our profession (as much as it is possible) will not hurt or confuse the people to whom we have a definite, true responsibility. Families will never accept your absence for long periods, simply because it is beyond their comprehension that anything could be more important than the family being together. They are, of course, quite right. But the demands that this industry puts on artistes are many and there are a million reasons for going home. The rusty creaking limbs of our passion will almost break in our frustration and our stepped-on, bruised fingers will slip from time to time amid utter financial despair. We are sometimes rocked and stunned by rejection, unfair criticism and lies. After all, we are only people with the same hearts and love as all others. Even the most successful among us will struggle in the sticky web of the glamour, the industry pulling you one way and your family pulling the other. The industry will want you to remain successful and your family will want you to survive. They are our safety net and those of us who try to work without them are at great risk. Elvis Presley fell and a cushion woven from millions of dollars couldn't save him. I have seen the passing of great friends, my old stable-mate Jimi Hendrix stumbled and staggered through his short life, tearing every emotion from his soul. Tears and anger belching from every fibre of his being. He used the artificial props of dangerous folly to help him keep pace with the hellish demands of the people who depended on him to make their living.

'If only, if only, I say to thee, thy net were made of love of love'. Gone is my dear friend Marc Bolan, whose pace thundered through every day he lived. Songs that touched the most remote of youthful hearts remain while this painter of people's joy has been tossed into oblivion and eternity. The reaching arms of his millions of fans and the love of his wife and child failed to grasp him from the hands of angels.

Paul Kossoff, the great guitar player from the band 'Free', lay in my home unconscious from a cocktail of drugs and frustration. He phoned me at 1.00 o'clock in the morning, apparently abandoned by a band he was doing some work with. He told me that he was at a motorway service station on the M6 motorway. He had no idea which one, only that it was somewhere near Stoke-on-Trent. I could tell that he was in a bit of a state and, after telling him to remain in the telephone booth until I got there, I set out to find him.

Sixty miles and three service areas later I found my little pal in a pathetic condition. After a couple of years of high success a soul-destroying schedule of back-breaking travelling, breathtaking guitar playing and mind-spinning adulation, this young man delved into the temporary relief of cold-blooded killer drugs. His meeting with this impostor of rest engraved his signature on the worst contract this industry can offer you. His own death warrant, signed in his own blood. From that moment young

Paul Kossoff was doomed. He had cut the rope that held his family safety net and put himself into the hands of pushers - careless, hateful people who think of nothing but the disgusting opulence that their evil trade can provide for them. The magnificent efforts of Paul's broken hearted father, David Kossoff, who so selflessly tried to save his son, were futile against this monster of death. Soon after this episode Paul Kossoff died from a heart attack, the legacy of his sad indulgence.

To blame our industry for this is rather like blaming the game of football for violence. These phenomena are all over our society and everyone's children are vulnerable to them. People in all walks of life die every day from drugs and violence and someone is to blame. We all have to look further than the victims. They were too young to be responsible for their own demise. We are only God's children. Unfortunately we all foolishly look to be protected by people who are no stronger than ourselves.

I watched through the airport window as a plane with H. Cain on board left Nashville for England. I felt a little sad as the jet disappeared into the clouds and hoped my good friend had a safe journey home. I had a couple of drinks in the airport bar and made a silent toast to the friends who had helped me to be there, to the people who had listened to my music and to the people I hoped my new music might reach. Here's to you my dears, whoever and wherever you are. There is a song in me and it's for you, only for you.

A few weeks later I was summoned to the Jack Clement's Studio. We were ready to begin my first Country music album. Larry Butler sent a car for me and as we drove down Music City Row I felt good. I had been waiting for a long time for this moment and I was loving every moment of it.

The band was set up when I arrived at the Studio and Larry introduced me to them. The best moment for me was meeting the Jordannaires. These singers had sung with Elvis Presley for many years and now they were about to sing with Froggy. Wow! What a thought!

Everybody was really kind and helpful. They could see that I was experienced in recording but they could also see that I was unfamiliar with the Nashville technique, which is wholly unique to Music City, Tennessee.

I am a quick learner and very flexible to the approaches of other styles. I couldn't teach these people anything and I knew it from the word go. I (in their words) 'listened up now' and found myself enjoying what I was 'listening up' to. I was ecstatic when Larry told me to take my place at the microphone standing in the middle of the Jordannaires. I thought to myself 'Elvis has stood and sung with these same people'. Even though I was the shortest man in the group I felt ten feet tall. After all, there can't be many people from the back streets of Birmingham, England who had stood and sung their own song with Elvis Presley's backing group. It's unforgivable but I felt rather proud of myself.

When I was a young teenager out with my mates at the local hops, listening, and idolising Elvis as we all did, I couldn't have imagined in my wildest dreams that one day I would be doing this.

It's funny how life moves. My first job, after leaving school at the age of 15, was as a delivery boy for a George Mason's Grocery Store. In the following few years I had been a roofer, a pipe lagger, a car breaker, a brickyard barrow-runner, a bakery chef, borematic machine operator, a sheetmetal worker, a road surfacer and a stable boy. Then there was music.

How lucky we were in our young days. We were able to try many things in order to find what we felt we were good at. We were able to search for something that we could enjoy doing and be content that we had found our place, a place in which we felt we belonged, a foundation from which we could start our own families with someone new, a genuine hope for our future. An opportunity to join other people in the dizzy moments of love and dreams. How sad and different for the young of today. They are expected to show respect for material things which they feel they can never own. Their noses are pressed against the window of other people's doings with the inner despair that they might not be able to join in. The passing of their day is accompanied by other, even younger, confused beings who, like they, are walking in limbo. They are forced to live on unwanted giros with their ears full of criticism of their kind. If they remain quiet and passive they are called lazy. If they scream in anger they are called violent and ungrateful. They witness the leaders of the world lying and glorying in slaughter. They perceive the empty promises of politicians who have knocked their parents for six with sweeping changes that tear down human dignity and replace it with raw abandonment, resentment and walls of unscalable insult. They watch, as the parents they still need become themselves needy. Before their puzzled eyes are the elderly, who are so abominably treated that it is difficult for them to understand what care means. The authorities, who are supposed to stand for something and protect people, become an enigma and so become, to young minds, their enemies. Bad housing, unemployment, bad policing, under-funded health care, lack of concern for the old and handicapped, blame cast upon the innocent for political justification, glory for the money maker and contempt for the technologically overtaken craftsmen. Visions for the children? The young are a multitude. We must hope that they are not turned to wolves, for if wolves they become, where then will lie the blame?

Seven days and the album was complete. I had made my recording transition into Country music. I had come to know Nashville and although I was looking forward to going home I knew I would miss this great city.

I had learned a lot about the American Country music making machine. The emphasis leaned firmly towards lyric and there was (as far as I could see) an honest delivery in performance. Dynamic and yet simple. All of these attributes are married to every type of existing rhythm and strong melody you can imagine. In short very difficult to create. But I felt that a challenge like this could be very fulfilling.

I wondered what Mervyn Conn had in store for me in order that we could be introduced to British Country music fans. I said my goodbyes to the people I had met, and left America. My life was about to change completely but I had no idea how. this was another beginning. My introduction card was my album 'Southern Fried Frog'.

R.I.P.
In Memory of Billy Paul

Billy Paul You Were Simply Great.

H. & Lynn Cain with Superstar Mark.

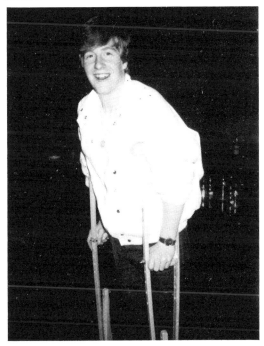

Frog and Radio Presenter John Mier, enjoying one of John's awful jokes.

Central TV Presenter Bob Warman and his wife, at Froggies Town Hall Show.

Chapter fifteen

MADE IN ENGLAND

After changing planes in Chicago I finally reached Heathrow Airport. A taxi to Euston Station and Intercity 125 to Brum - I was home.

Although I lived in this town I was still homeless so I rang my old friend H. Cain. I had not told anyone that I was coming back so he was surprised to hear from me. Within 20 minutes he arrived to pick me up. If the whole world were to turn against me H. Cain and his family would share all they had with me. Strong we are as strong shall be, strong the Earth holds such as thee'.

Don Arden and Mervyn Conn asked us to be at Don's London office to discuss the promotion and release of our album. It was a promising meeting with the album being highly praised by all of the executive staff at Jet Records. The promotion of a record at a major record company involves almost all of the Company's staff; first of all the Chairman (in this case Don Arden) will call an A & R meeting. This involves the attendance of the heads of each department. They will be invited to offer their ideas using their own individual knowledge as to how the product will be promoted. The head of A & R at any record company, is the main man. It is his decision whether a record is released or not. All of the other departments are collectively his responsibility. They will look to him for their budgets. He is the sort of 'Chancellor of the Exchequer'.

His length of stay in this capacity at any one time is about the same as a real Chancellor, thus being the nature of this very precarious industry. Hits and misses mean, to them, job or no job. Men like Don Arden and Mervyn Conn tolerate no one. You either do good or get out. No frills, no fancy sad goodbyes, no golden handshake. Just 'piss off', and that's that!

Everyone in our industry knows the strength and they all work with great humour within the uncertainty of their tomorrow. There are some people who dabble in this business but they are never any good at it and they are the ones who squeal like pigs when they find out the realities of this work.

The publicity man responsible for advertising and newspaper write-ups, the plugger responsible for the radio plays and TV slots, the art designer responsible for packaging, general logo, posters and shop window display, the distributor responsible for the record getting to every shop, window display, the liaison man responsible for the artiste's contact with the Company in order to get the artiste's full co-operation and attendance at all pre-arranged functions to do with promotion, Mervyn Conn, the promoter and tour organiser, Don Arden who is paying for it all, Raymond Froggatt who wrote the songs and will front their performance, H. Cain responsible for the musicians and the A & R manager who will get the bollocking if it all goes wrong, sat around a table to discuss the release of my album 'Southern Fried Frog'. I knew everyone at that meeting and, with the exception of Mervyn, I had worked with them all for years. I knew that they all wanted me to succeed, Don and Mervyn for their financial commitment to each other and the others because they all had witnessed the years and effort I had put into my attempts to make it. They were all going to do their absolute utmost to help me but once I got out on the road it was all going to be down to me. I would have to reach the people in my own way. No matter how much money Don and Mervyn are prepared to spend I knew it could never buy a place in the hearts of grown-up people. The hype in our industry will work if you are aiming a good looking boy or girl at youngsters. It's been happening for years and will continue to happen. It is not illegal, it's just temporary. The only losers are the good looking boys and girls. Some of them will survive but most, sadly, fade because of the tragedies I have mentioned in the book.

Our album would be launched with a nationwide series of press receptions at major hotels in every city of Great Britain. National and local reporters would be invited to indulge in good wine in opulent surroundings in return for favourable reviews of this new Country artiste and his Nashville-made album.

I can say now, with the benefit of hindsight, that the record company approached this venture in such a way that the operation was totally futile. There were representatives from all the local papers in every area we visited. These are important people but they have a problem which is no fault of theirs. It's just that space in local newspapers reserved for music is very limited and the reporter is obliged to feature star names. In the space left over, the editor and readers will hope to see music and bands reviewed that have a local interest. I was neither a star or local, so the best I could hope for was a four-line review of my album. With the best will in the world the local reporters could do little more for me. On a national level there were reporters from the Melody Maker, the NME and other pop mags, but these people are not interested in promoting Country music of any kind, let alone Country music recorded by an artiste who was made in England. It wasn't because the recording company were stupid, it was because they simply didn't know who the reporters from the Country music press were. They had no idea that an invitation to local Country music presenters (who had radio programmes that reached the very heart of the fans) would have been better than a thousand reporters from pop mags.

The Company had launched my album as they would have launched a rock album and inadvertently they missed their market.

Mervyn was angry and disappointed that they had not sought the expertise of his company in this venture. He was much more qualified and knowledgeable to set up this affair than anyone. The trouble with that is the probability of political conflict arising between two major companies, when one tells the other that they could do the job better. It would be like Don Arden telling Mervyn Conn that he could promote the Wembley

Festival, it's just food for battle. The sad thing is that because of this my album had a bad start.

Mervyn Conn had hoped that by the time he introduced us to the fans at Wembley Festival we would have been mentioned in the Country press. As it was, not even the press or the radio presenters knew who the hell I was. As far as the fans were concerned I might just as well come from China for all they knew.

H. Cain put a band together and we were ready for our first appearance in front of the British Country music fans at Wembley. We were asked to play for fifteen minutes.

We were due on stage at 5.00 o'clock on Bank Holiday Monday

afternoon. Wally Wyton was to introduce me on stage. He asked me how I would like to be introduced and, quite honestly, I didn't know what he meant. I answered by saying 'Say anything that comes to mind'. I sensed his displeasure and understandably so, because he had never heard of me either. He said 'Well, what have you been doing?' The only thing I could think of was that I had just composed a song for Shirley Bassey. He rolled his eyes and went on stage.

As Wally addressed the audience they applauded and he gave me my first introduction in Country music. 'Ladies and Gentlemen, I have to introduce an artiste to you who has just told me that he has written a song for Shirley Bassey'. Sarcastically he added 'I thought now there's another fine Country music achievement. Here he is - Raymond Froggatt'.

The crowd were polite and a little confused. They listened to my songs, 'All Because of You', 'Roly', 'Teach Me' and 'Always Goodbye'. Our applause was not over-generous but it was polite, warmly given and possibly all we deserved on that day.

I had just been introduced to a completely different audience, a new set of people who had a purist's faith in the kind of music they liked. I felt that I must try and deliver my songs in a true way so that my music would be accepted with the same enthusiasm that it is performed. I knew instinctively that this would not be easy, but I thought to myself that these people are not from Mars, they are just like me; ordinary folk from the towns, cities and villages of Great Britain; my own countrymen and women who cry, laugh, bleed, love, hate, hope, dream, win, lose and hang precariously from the threads of their time. The windows of their lives are sometimes stained with the tears and grime of ordinary days. Their wishes are blown like autumn leaves down the avenue of love, bouncing and turning towards the hands of care.

'Catch me 'ere I fall, for I am only songs. Songs I have to give thee are wrapped in air. So many are the ears and far the distance can be. I shall still and ever follow thee'.

Almost immediately I fell into controversy. My innocent connection with Mervyn Conn's Company was seen by the Country music fans and the media to be an unfair privilege given to someone who, to their minds, had not 'paid his dues', when in fact I had been an object of an inner business deal whereby I had been exchanged to another area of the industry for money.

I understood the concern of the British fans. After all they had their favourite British artistes and felt protective towards them. To their minds this simply wasn't fair. Here was an unknown singer about to support Tammy Wynette on a national tour and also represent Great Britain at the Nashville Fan Fair. It was all too much for the fans to accept. I felt also that it was the wrong way for me to begin my career in Country music. Much to Mervyn's disappointment I refused to go to Nashville.

The damage was done and I knew it would take me a long time to find the hearts and ears of these determined people. Anyway, I'm a good old stayer and so is H. Cain, so here we go again! The battles in existence are many fold, not just for us but for all people in every walk of life. And so there are days of falling hours, rising dawns, love of youth, trials of hope, songs of people. Follow the sun and under God we run. Take the hands of those you love. Calm words will cool the anxious feet of those who chase colours. We are clothed in the shadow of every chance of joy. The young shall find the same road of good fortune that carries us all.

Chapter sixteen

CHANGES FOR THE BETTER?

For anyone to begin a new area of life is very difficult, not only in music, but in all changes that come along in everybody's day at sometime or another. You and I have no control over the corners we turn. Even though we may want to go one way time's magnet will drag you screaming to the other. People have a lot to do with the journeys we make. Sometimes they simply fall out with you and sometimes you become a barrier. As I've grown I have constantly looked for change, but I have never wanted it thrust upon me. I must say I felt terribly abandoned by my recording company, because I knew that this was not only a career move, it was goodbye from everything and everyone I knew in the rock music area of our industry.

I had simply grown too old, without record success, and become 'in the way'. Those not knowing what to try with me next, sold me. It was a solution of a kind. It meant that I was still worth something in a monetary kind of way, but after their deal I was still only Froggy. Slowly the big wheels let me slip away into the confusion of not knowing the first thing that was going on.

Don Arden had finally let me go and I knew then that my recording days with a major recording company were over.

I had made records with almost every label in Great Britain, Europe and America. Although I had made (with my friend H. Cain) some of the (as far as the recording companies were concerned) finest works of our time, we hadn't moved the public enough to buy them and now we were outgrown by the business.

I never look to lay blame for failure at the door of anyone. It is too easy to do that. I have, however, looked for reasons just in case it was something I had been doing wrong. I have made, and had released, 60 single records in my time, but I have never been able to go into a store and buy my own record. They haven't ever been there. It's plain that we have been let down many times in the distribution department. Although that can be disastrous for an artiste, it is only one hurdle that can trip you up. There are many cogs that have to be set in motion, as I have mentioned already in this testament.

First of all, of course, you have to write a hit song, and that is my fault so I share the blame with others and leave it at that. I had now been given another challenge - to take my songs to Country music people. Mervyn Conn had divorced is association with Don Arden but he kept his commitment to us and informed us that he would do as much as he could (as far as it was possible) to lend a hand in our effort. He stood by his word.

We were asked to support the major American artistes on their tours. We had supported many times so we knew exactly what to do; never to try consciously to upstage the star. This is his or her audience. You are there to open the show, not to try and steal it. If you foolishly try that the audience will know and be indifferent to you. There are many who fall chasing this folly. If you complement the stars then their audience will compliment you. The star will feel comfortable with your contribution and become interested in what you are. If a good rapport is noticed between you and the star, then the newspaper reporters will want to talk to you. It can be really nice supporting a top star because there is never any pressure on you. All you have to be, is early and professional. They money is not good but the feeling is great.

In this day and age it is very refreshing to work with 'working people'. By that I mean people who realise that show business is work and we who toil in it are totally dependant upon the people who pay to see us. I have known, and still know, people who consider themselves to be special human beings simply because they can sing or perform in some way. Their opinion of themselves goes beyond confidence. It is sometimes downright smugness, and they are positively sickening. Also, they are an insult to our industry. Most of the big stars that I have had the pleasure of working with have been superb in the manner in which they conduct themselves, showing professional humility and gratitude to the people they depend on. It's not difficult, it's just a matter of remembering who you really are.

I have employed musicians who feel that they should change everything to suit themselves. They forget that I have another six people to consider in the administration of a full band. All of my players have always been paid whether they work or not. They are never asked to contribute from their earnings anything towards expenses, which include telephone bills, agency booking fees, company tax, stationery and postal costs, pa and lighting hire, transport fuel and maintenance costs, such as new tyres, services, food, hotel bills, theatre hire and advertising costs. Whenever their holidays fall they are paid fully and the expense of a replacement player is paid for in full by the Company. They are picked up and dropped off at their doors. Their jobs are as secure as is possible in this precarious business I have had musicians who count seats and look at the entry fee, add it up and then think that one fifth of the takings belongs to them without a single thought of how the concert has been organised or the cost of the administration of it. They have caused rumblings of discontent by trying to gather support among the others, thus causing a split. Between commonsense and stupidity there they sit watching what goes on after they have done their worst. They always lose, and take with them the snide manner in which they spend their lives. Their names are not worth mentioning in this book or any other. They have not got the courage, nor is there a pen full of poison enough for them to write one themselves. They have forgotten the people they play to; the very people who pay us all. Shame on them!

You see, the villains are not always in the hierarchy of our business, there are many who live and play among the musicians.

When I first arrived on the Country music scene in Britain there was a great resentment against me. Although I had been in the entertainment world for over twenty years this was the first time I had experienced genuine hatred for being who I am. The people who vanguarded this campaign did not know me yet they persisted in their attempts to kick me off the world!

It took me a long time to realise that they are only a few, but they are the type who write to trade papers at every opportunity to harm me. It doesn't seem to matter to them that they are attempting to take the livelihood from my musicians and taking the bread from their children's mouths. Musicians are only working people with families to support. I am not Saddam Hussein - I am Raymond Froggatt; just a singer in a band. I don't know what harm I can do to the planet by being only that.

Quite recently I read a piece of libel concerning my non-appearance at the Inverness Festival. Not only was this delightful epistle steeped in spite by calling me a 'so called singer', but it threatened my fans with verbal violence if they were to set foot north of the border wearing my name. Having hundreds of Scottish friends I find it difficult to imagine any Scot verbally abusing any child, elderly lady or family, for wearing a jacket of their choice. The only thing that this letter achieved was to insult the fine decency of the Scottish people. The reason that we didn't appear was the fact that H. Cain had conjunctivitis (a bad infection of the eyes) and the poor bugger could hardly see, let alone make the journey to Inverness! Knowing my enemies as I do and H. Cain being the extremely nice, inoffensive man he is, I decided to take the blame, thus protecting him from the victim's slander, which I am now immune to. It makes me physically sick to write about these people so I'll skip along and just let them know that, after fifteen years of their sniping, whoever they are, it makes not the slightest mark on my armour that there are people in the world who will never accept my contribution to music. My life is built of many thousands of bright and dark moments in the industry and outside of it. I have never done anything in half measures. My commitment to life is a waterfall of mistakes and instant decisions. So you see I am bound to make enemies, but I have to make my way in the world as I see it. I can say however, quite categorically, that I have not aimed spite at anyone in my entire life. I see spite as a pointless exercise that can only bring turmoil and pained spirit to the very deepest part of your own soul. It is ridiculous for any of us to imagine that our personal opinions will alter the minds and directions of someone else. As there are people who will always hate me, there will also be those who will rain love on my efforts. I see nothing extra special in me other than the fact that I write songs and sing them. I cannot even do that alone. I can only direct my songs towards the ears of strangers, in the company of others. I can only ever be Raymond Froggatt in my own band, but my musicians can be part of another the very next day. I am constantly aware of this and so I front all of our doings with love. This is the only way I know. In fifteen years on the Country scene I have performed 4,500 times and missed 23 shows through illness or other unforeseen problems, so no one can be well known enough to slander by never turning up.

I am a serious professional and I take my industry just as seriously as I take breath. I have not ever stayed at home when it has been possible for me to sing. An audience is like a waiting kiss to me. I have been, and shall always be, kissed many times. So there!!

So, to you who write in a negative manner of others, I would urge you to write favourably of the people you love. They, like me, need all the help we can get. For without you our industry offers us nothing. To be understanding and kind is quite beautiful. So it remains that all rest and peace shall dwell in the hearts of the calm.

Know who your enemies are. Understand them, but never ever forget them for they will always be waiting. Show business is fantastic to be involved in so when the odd mud ball comes flying in my direction I just side step and let it pass on by. Criticism is very import to us all to my mind. Sometimes when criticism is made in a knowledgeable way it can be quite helpful. None of us can be sure of how we can make improvements. We live too close to what we are doing to be fully aware of the visual mechanics of our performing. Constructive suggestion, I'm sure is welcomed by us all providing it isn't laced with the poison of someone's personal opinions of us as people, be they on the derisive side, or the other.

I have too many scars for dagger points to find space enough to pierce. Stay thy wrath, for tis only thy kiss I desire. All things are in splendour to us all though the way be narrow my love and yours shall ever walk apart. How sad. Never mind, it's only life my dears!

Our first tour was to be supporting Tammy Wynette, a delightful young lady with a quite beautiful nature. We were made very welcome among the American troupe and soon became professional friends. We knew, through our experience, exactly what was expected of us and remained invisible, though always available, throughout the entire itinerary of the carefully constructed performances.

It was difficult to measure our responses from the Country audiences because, although there were a lot of Country music fans at each venue, it's fair to say that there were equally as many fans who were not fully Country music followers, but were particularly fond of Tammy Wynette, her goodself being what is known in the business as a crossover artiste.

We were well received but, as a support artiste, this is never a true yardstick as to your future popularity. We were just a small part of a very nice evening out for a lot of people. Unless we were ever working with

Tammy Wynette it was unlikely that half of them would ever see us again and because of our bad start and unfortunate publicity the other half didn't care either way.

Rob Zurazki was working as a concert organiser for Mervyn Conn at the time. We had known him since his university days when he was a 'social sec' and responsible for booking the bands for the various shindigs all students enjoy so much. We have always been good friends and now he is 'the man' at the Bournemouth Centre complex. We are still able to keep in touch. Indeed, we put our show in there once a year at his pleasure. I am very fond of Rob. It was in these early days that his spirit and advice was so instrumental in me being able to conquer my latest dilemma. It was difficult for me to know how to go about finding the audience that I was supposed to entertain. Don Arden, having cast me into Mervyn's hands, and Mervyn only interested in the huge festivals and tours, it was impossible for me to get to know the Country people at grass roots.

Rob suggested that I should try to get into the Country Music clubs. It was like starting a new school and the first thing to do was to look for friends, find the bullies and either keep out of their way or fight them. I took them on in the manner of my upbringing.

My memories of childhood form a strong resilience towards conflict. I have never been weak in character. I have been pushed from pillar to post in the roughest area of Birmingham and grown up with people who would bite your face off for the cast-off shoe from a British Rail horse.

Cherry Wood Road in Bordesley Green was a bomb site; a gift from the Luftwaffe. We who lived round there would dig, run over, climb, search, build dreams and throw the bricks that had once formed the home of many a young wife and mother. These piles of rubble, into which the sounds of crying babies, the arguments of young married couples, the protest of reluctant bedtime children had echoed around rooms of a one-time family home. The oilcloth, now torn and flapping in the dust and wind, once covered the splintered boards of a living-room floor. The lead pipes, that once spewed water to wash dirty faces at teatime, were how hanging lianas waving in a jungle where Tarzan had a Birmingham accent.

If, like a shell, you would hold a brick to your ear, the sound of creaking doors, barking dogs, the smell of blood, the hopeless tears of a family whose daddy didn't come home, would be heard instead of the sea.

I stayed most of the time with our Gran Rosie Sullivan. The group of houses still left standing formed a yard. Four toilets, shared by all were joined to a washroom we all called the Brew-house.

The Brew-house contained a copper boiler embedded in brick with a fire hole beneath to heat the water.

One morning the circular wooden lid was half covering the boiler top to let the steam out and David Miller fell in and died. I wonder what he would have grown up to be? Emma Lamb lived next door to our Gran and some of my uncles would entertain her from time to time. Betty Teague lived across the yard. She was a huge woman and I can still remember her huge white legs with fire burns up the inside of her shins. She always seemed to be hanging washing out. None of our washing ever looked very clean. When I think back, I suppose it was difficult when there

wasn't any such thing as washing powder. Once Gran used to scrape slithers of green soap into the boiler.

Rosie Sullivan had seventeen kids and when I stopped there all of my aunts had gone off to be married. The house had two bedrooms and our Gran lived there all her married life. It beats me how they all grew up in such a small place, but they did.

Our Grandad was a bit of an old bastard. He was always pissed. Most nights he would come home and punch all the panels out of the doors and fall asleep in front of the fire-grate. Rosie sometimes used to drag him up the old winding staircase by the feet and let him go when she got to the top! He could never remember why he found himself on the kitchen floor in a heap the next day.

The only time I can remember that he had a job was when he was a conductor on the trams. But one day he pissed off with all the fares at the terminus and ended up in the nick for twelve months. 'The dear boy'.

I'll never understand why they called our street 'Cherry Wood Road' because nothing like a tree was ever seen; just rows of terraced houses, the Co-op Horse Yard and Mulliners Factory at the end of the street. Mrs Bennett's outdoor nestled neatly in the middle of the poverty and all of the purchases were on the strap 'till the weekend.

I would regularly take Gran's pop bottle with a screw top, down to Mrs Bennet's. 'A pint and a stick for Gran please on the strap'. The shell of the mild ale rushing from pump to jug, and then jug to bottle, seemed like another world to me. I could just about get my finger tips on to the highly polished bar, and watch the huge beer pumps being pulled forward and then back. The froth spilled over the neck of the bottle, a quick wipe down with the bar cloth, then 'Hold it tight and don't run back'. 'OK Mrs Bennett. Thank you'.

Gran would take the bottle. 'Did you say thank you?' 'Yes, Gran'. She rubbed the inside of her wrist across her mouth and took a swig straight from the bottle. The bottle was then placed by the side of her chair as she pushed the inquisitive ginger mongrel dog (our Prince) out of the way. 'Get under you bastard you stink blind'. He always thought his name was Bastard. I was the only one who called him Prince. Prince shuffled under the table in the bay window and lay down. Just as we knew what please and thank you mean, Prince knew the importance of 'get under'. For us kids and Prince not to respond to either demand would mean the order of the boot. Our Gran was as tough as nails. She had to be, like all of our Grans in those days, to bring a houseful of kids up without assistance, a drinking man for a husband, and all the wear that lines the beautiful ladies in our lives

If I had half a chance or the wish of kings, I would take our Gran to have her hair done. In her entire life she only ever combed it with water from a dribbling tap and parted it on the side. Just a wash and brush-up.

'Raymond, take the batteries out of the wireless to the shop for charging up. Tell them I want them done for this afternoon to listen to Mrs Dale's Diary with Granny Smith'. Granny Smith lived across the yard in the corner. She always dressed in long black clothes and never came out of her house. She was ninety then, and her husband had been killed in the Boer War. They didn't have time to make any kids. Our Gran was her only friend.

Our Gran was always telling me stories about the people she had known and I was in awe of the bright sparkle in her eyes as she spoke to me about her days.

There was 'Conkie Whallop', a big woman who lived round our way. During the Blitz her job was to guard the Midland Bank on the Bordesley Green from looters. One morning the Bank had received a direct hit and all they found of 'Conkie' was her gun and tin hat.

I'd sit on Gran's lap with my head on her breast and listen for ages to the stories of her family in Ireland, of her childhood and the dreams she followed in her colleen days.

She would whisper of the memories of Cork and the beautiful land she could still see beneath closed eyes. Nothing bounced off me. I believe now, when I'm looking back, the seeds of my life today in music were planted as I sat on Gran's knee where I shared thoughts.

As we all grew up and years passed by, the Council knocked our yard down. Granny Smith was gone, Prince had long ago died and they moved Gran to Hockley in Birmingham She was very old by now. She was frightened and alone in her heart. She died in a house she was unfamiliar with, in a place far from where she was born. She took with her the dreams and pictures of her hopes. The young girl who had skipped and played in the fields of County Cork has gone to heaven. Rest in peace Gran.

When you measure slander and spite against the bright sky of true life and precious people, the slander and spite counts for very little. There are no stories worth listening to when they are belched from a jealous heart. They are cobwebs in dark corners where for all the purpose of their birth they will drown in clouds in a place where the stars will never shine.

Very few Country clubs at first were interested in my performing for them. They considered that my music wasn't Country and that was that. There were a few however who were willing to take a risk and try it out. Although we were not fully accepted, people were not insulting towards us. Country fans are not the type to deliberately deride anyone.

My biggest problem was that I don't do any Country classic songs. Quite honestly I couldn't see the point. If it had been impossible for me to write my own songs I would have been glad to sing other people's material, but I felt it would be cheating my audience to simply sing songs that would get me out of trouble. I think if I had been a young Willie Nelson starting in Britain, I would have felt the same way. Our own music is important to the effort and no one would know if they like it or not if we didn't try.

I remember at one club I went to the toilet an stood by a chap who asked me if I would sing 'The Crystal Chandeliers' and, quite truly, I didn't know it. Although I was familiar with the song it was out of the question

He said to me 'call yourself a Country singer and don't know one of the best songs ever written? You're a waste of thirty bob'. I felt a bit hurt, but not for myself. I really wanted to entertain him It had disappointed me to think that because I didn't know it, I was a waste of his money.

Thinking back, I'm glad I didn't know it because I would probably have chickened out and sung it.

It was a slow process trying to win over the Country people, but everywhere I could feel a certain warmth coming through. Now and again some folk would ask if we had a record of a certain song. Sometimes we were asked to sing one of my songs as a request. Things were beginning to look up!

I used my experience to cope with the sad days and there were always the other British artistes to give you a boost. A lot of them admired my spirit in hanging on to what I believed it, and some of them began to sing some of my songs. A great compliment indeed. Even though I had written many songs for world stars, this gave me an extra special lift. It was a difficult area of music. The British Country artiste is a rare breed indeed. they work on a treadmill that is totally ignored by the music industry as a whole. The major labels are indifferent to Country music, not because they think it is rubbish, it's because they feel it will not generate enough money to make their interest worthwhile.

I have heard lots of records made by British Country artistes without the benefit of gian record companies and huge budgets, or the use of an ultra-modern sixty-four track computerised recording studio. They make as fine a job on records as I have heard, yet they are criticised about quality and production by people who have never been in a recording studio in their lives. I bleed for effort that is cut down and cheapened. I have seen and been a victim being a British artiste at the now defunct Wembley Festival.

Although the British Country fans give all the support we could ask for our treatment backstage was nothing short of humiliating. You would be hanging about all day without the slightest interest being taken in your welfare. Now and again organisers would show their faces to tell you 'You're on in three minutes - and don't stay on longer than eight minutes or you're for the high jump'. Then some fat overfed Yank who you've never heard of would come strolling in, spend three hours doing a sound check, complain about this and that and the other, then get on stage and make a right cock-up of it.

There are of course great and lesser artistes in Britain and America but whoever you are you deserve certain respect just for being there.

I remember doing a show there on the main stage and the reception we got from the British fans was tremendous. Throughout our part of the show the fans were on their feet waving Froggie scarves and singing along with every British home-grown song. At last we had made an impact on the occasion. It was a great moment and I felt it was an achievement for all of the British fans and also for the British artistes. Together we had made a success for all to see.

When the Country press released their magazines at the end of the month, quite rightly, it was full of the reports on the Wembley Festival. The report on our effort on the show went something like this:

'Then Froggatt hit the stage. He did his usual thing with the audience going wild, waving their scarves as if at a football match. What we can't understand is why anyone can get so enthusiastic over someone who's only ever reached the semifinal'.

Now, correct me if I'm wrong, but after thirty years in this business you can't call that criticism - it's downright bloody mindedness. I'm bound to say that, being an Aston Villa supporter, that if they reached the semifinal in any cup I would be very proud of them indeed. Not that it's likely they would be scoffed at by the tabloids for doing so ... In the light of that you can see what the British artiste is up against. If they thought that these comments would damage me they were as wrong as their review was.

cheap. I'm still here, and the people who their scarves - that's good enough for me. I'll see you literary geniuses at the final fighting for a ticket - you won't get one.

You have to try to stay calm in all areas of insult but I'm sure you know that at times it can be very hard when you are being attacked by faceless enemies. It's a natural impulse to defend yourself and I'm no different to anyone else. Somehow though, I manage to cope and keep fighting back, armed with songs.

Chapter
seventeen

HOYT 'N' ROSIE, AND LETTERS IN GOLD

What a strange exciting life we lead with all of the turns, corners and fences. How different the days. Should a way be closed another lane is stepped on with the confidence of fools. What rogues are born of saints for a turn of time. The magic of a moment felt deep, from eye to eye. The momentary strike of passion as the pace of your heart skips. You can almost feel the blood. I shall bleed, there is no doubt of that.

My God! Why did I have to fall in love with this business? Couldn't I have just found it as something to play with, toy with it, laugh with it, touch, kiss and tire of it? What then, this minstrel, is there after all has passed? By all means bury me but spare my songs for they are innocent children.

Hoyt Axton is one of the most talented people I've ever known. He's a songwriter, singer, actor and all round entertainer. This totally unaffected star has made hit Hollywood movies, written world hit songs and taken his band all over the world.

I was fortunate enough to support his British tour with 'Rosemarie'. It was a joyful journey of the major theatres in Great Britain, put together by Mervyn Conn. To work with Hoyt is an enormous pleasure. His marvellous humour and ordinary charm is infectious in the extreme. His band and other fellow travellers from America were an extension of his own memorable nature.

We travelled in the tour bus from north to south, never missing a sweet shop. Hoyt had a passion for Cadbury Fudge bars. I shudder to think how many he accommodated but I'm sure he won't mind me saying he had plenty of room in his six foot three, over twenty-five stone frame to keep the Cadbury conveyor belts going for a week.

I learned a lot from Hoyt. He always calls me 'Raymond Ribbit-Ribbit-Ribbit'. His style and his laid-back approach to this industry is inspiring. His tremendous songwriting talents were as natural and economical as it is possible to be. No pretentious lines of something he didn't know about. Hoyt Axton is a true born talent from the womb of the woman who wrote 'Heartbreak Hotel' for Elvis. I asked his mother how she felt about writing that song and she just replied 'Well Froggie it paid the rent for a while'.

On this tour Rosemarie was terrific. She is a very funny lady who can mix her stage presence with comedy and serious performance. We all had great fun with Rosie and I mean that in the nicest possible way. she's a true professional and works very hard. She goes it alone and that takes some doing in this business. Good luck Rosie, always. See you soon.

Shortly after this tour was over I met Hoyt at the Peterborough Festival. Like all of the other British artistes I wasn't allowed into the VIP tent, so Hoyt stayed outside with me. Then, just before Kris Kristoffersen went on stage, someone came up to inform us that Kris didn't want anyone at the back of the stage while he was performing. Hoyt replied 'Well we sure as hell ain't gonna be standin in front of it'. Nice one Hoyt.

I was always asking Hoyt to take a drink with me on tour but each time he declined the offer, until the final concert in Kendal, Cumbria, he didn't say anything, he just picked me up under his arm, carried me into the hotel bar and sat me on a stool. He asked the barman to get a pint glass and fill it with a shot from every optic in the bar. I watched, puzzled and silent as Hoyt lifted the concoction to his mouth and drank it down in one slug. 'Now, Raymond Ribbit-Ribbit-Ribbit; about that drink'. I sank into humble silence as my big old friend roared with laughter. His final line was 'Work first - play later, ya hear?' 'Gotcha Hoyt'.

Like us all, I've learned many lessons from friends. When I was fifteen I took up boxing. Our family have always been a boxing family. My father was the ABA Bantam Weight Champion of Great Britain and my Uncle, Joe Froggatt, was the British European and Lightweight Champion. Quite naturally I had the yearning to follow in their footsteps. I started fighting for Fishers Boxing Club in Birmingham. My trainer was Jackie Simson, the Flyweight Champion of 'Britain and the Armed Forces'. He was a terrific scrapper, a small fellow with huge ears. He had all the skill in the world and the aggression to go with it. He told me: 'See these ears, son?' (I was fifteen and laughed a bit.) 'A lot of blokes have took the piss out of them but not one of them could lay a glove on them'. I was a natural scrapper but you have to learn (not to be hit) in the fight game. The first lesson is self-defence. All I wanted to do was pile in there, caution to the wind. Most unwise. One can get severely knocked about in the process of throwing a single punch.

Johnny Prescott started fighting at the same time as me and it was obvious that he was going to be a contender. His terrific fights with Billy Walker are legendary. John had everything. He was a great looking kid so his charisma was immediate food for the girls. John loves the ladies, and who can argue with that? We have been pals since we were kids. The last time I saw John was at the Lord Mayor of Birmingham's Council Rooms where we attended a banquet in honour of the hundred years' birthday of Birmingham City. The City awarded a hundred people (one for each year of the City's birth) for their contribution to the City's fame. Johnny Prescott, Raymond Froggatt and Pat Roach were among politicians and sports personalities to receive our honours. The three musketeers Pat Roach called us!

The three of us were called to the table of dignitaries to accept our gold medals and scrolls. Three men from the back streets of Brum would go down on the Roll of Honour board printed in gold, mounted in the Council Chambers for ever. Pat became a wrestler and actor, John a heavyweight champion boxer, with yours truly, a singer and writer of songs. From back streets and scrapyards to letters in gold.

It's only time and where it takes you. Everybody's name is printed in gold somewhere. Every step taken by the weariest soul leaves the mark of their passing.

When I go across to Bridgnorth, near the river where I live, I think of Lou Clark now living in America. I imagine him as a child riding the cliff railway to get to his home in High Town. The same doors I walk through screech and clank in the same way they always did. The legs of friends have stepped over the same iron rail. The hands young, then older, passed a ticket through the small glass hole with the same words 'Thank you', uttered a million times. The same steel cable, black with grease and patterned with dandelion seeds has hauled and hauls the dreamers still.

Lou Clark, Len Ablethorpe and H. Cain's names are also printed in gold, not in the Council Chambers of Birmingham but on the scroll I carry always in my heart.

I gave up boxing after several beltings. Jackie Simson told me that I lacked aggression and I would have done better if every time I hit a kid with a good blow I didn't keep saying 'Are you all right mate?' I still love to watch the sport. I'm going to see a local boy, Richie Woodall, fight for the Commonwealth Middleweight title soon. He looks a great prospect and reminds me a little of Johnny Prescott. As long as he doesn't ask his opponent if he's 'All right mate' I think he'll win. I hope he can pull it off anyway - it's great to have some to support for whatever they do.

Chapter eighteen

A PROPER JOB

The school I first attended was in Paget Road, Birmingham. I remember little about it except that there were no desks or chairs. We all sat on a huge straw mat around the teacher. There was a sheet on the wall with small pockets sewn on to it with a number painted on each one. This was to put our sandwiches in on our arrival.

I was pretty thick throughout my school days and I was always in the lower classes. The only thing I liked was having stories read to us.

Even in those days I was a bit of a loner. I can always remember we moved house a lot. We were always lodging here and there. Our mom used to tell me that I would tear wallpaper and she would stick it back up with condensed milk before we were thrown out. I still move house a lot now. I suppose it's something to do with the habit of it.

When mom got married again we lived at number 2 Anerley Grove, Kingstanding, Birmingham. It was the beginning of a sort of settling down period. We had three moves after that. The first to 97 Cooksey Lane, and then to 534 Kings Road, all in Kingstanding. We stayed at 534 until I left home.

There were three schools in my life from our move to Anerley Grove - 'Kingland Road Juniors', 'Aldridge Comprehensive' and finally 'Kingsrise Seniors'. I can't tell you much about those days because they were all so uneventful. I learned the basics of education and once won a prize for writing a story about a river pike who ate everyone else in the river. He then got lonely and starved to death. I must have been having a premonition of my future involvement with Don Arden.

When I finally left school my life really began. I loved the freedom that came with a job. My first place of employment was at 'George Masons' a grocer's store. My first task was to take the Christmas decorations down. I was issued a white coat and apron and began to earn my own living. What a joy! Three pounds and one penny a week! My hours were 9 'till 5.30 each day and 9 'till 1 o'clock on Saturdays. I had the shop delivery bike to travel to and from work. I gave Mom thirty bob keep and had thirty bob to myself. I was loaded.

I liked the girls at the shop and the manager, Fred Shepard, taught me all there is to know about boning, jointing and cutting up bacon pigs. Sometimes I even got the chance to serve the customers. I was beginning to become interested in people. I found them fun and I saw the lovely ordinariness of them. Every Friday I would deliver the groceries to the better-off customers. One lady, Mrs Round, was our best customer. Her bill came to over five pounds a week. It used to astonish me that someone could spend that much on grub.

Our shop was the old fashioned kind. There were two long counters each side and three different types of scales along each counter. The food was stacked right to the ceiling on huge oak shelves at the rear of each counter. Sugar and rice, flour and biscuits, all came loose and would be weighed at the customer's request. The blue bags for the sugar hung on grass hooks. The bacon slab, full of dry cured, plain and smokey rashers, joints, hams and parsley, looked like Christmas fare all the year round. I can still smell the wonderful aroma of that store. Not only was it a service, it was also a work of art. From the door the inside looked like an old master's painting.

It wasn't long before progress came to visit us. We were going to be turned into a self-service shop. None of us knew what that was. It was a new idea and the beginning of the present day superstore had begun. After eighteen months I left, never to see the people who were my first workmates ever again. I wonder if some of them come to see us work in music now. I bet they wold never think that the scruffy young cheeky kid they once knew, is me.

This period in my life was typical of a teenager of the Fifties. It was around eight years before I got started in the music industry, and a career in show business was the furthest thing from my mind.

Like all youngsters I found my mates and became part of a gang. I was still doing a bit of boxing but when the chance came to go out with the lads or train, it was no contest. Our gang members were as follows:-

BEFORE		AFTER
Bricklayer	Tony 'Fatty' Wayne	RIP
Pipe Lagger	Frank 'Nankie' Bird	Pipe Lagger
Draughtsman	Keith 'Benji' Bedwood	Car Dealer
Draughtsman	Billy 'Dagwood' Rose	RIP
Pipe Lagger	Raymond 'Bog Roll' Froggatt	Singer
Pipe Fitter	Roy 'Sexy' Sale	Postman
RAF	Roy 'Gov' O'Grady	Retired Stock-holder-Steel
Rag Man	Ernie 'Spoint' O'Grady	RIP
Pipe Lagger	Tony 'Stratta' Stratford	Pipe Lagger
Pipe Fitter	Colin 'Oscar' Osbourn	Factory Worker (cars)
Pipe Fitter	Alan 'Bookie' Page	Salesman (steel)
Rag Man	Barry 'Bazmoz' Morris	Scrap Merchant
Pipe Fitter	Johnny 'Mac' Macathey	Pipe Fitter

At first we didn't have a car between us and, anyway, some of us were not yet old enough to have a licence. We went everywhere on the bus. Everyone of this motley crew looked old enough to get into a pub; so like every kid I've ever known, we started drinking at an early age.

The Jungle Expresso Bar in Snow Hill, Birmingham was our late night haunt. Many is the fracas that took place under God's heaven in that place of ill repute. Always game for a scrap, we were accommodated many times. Not a single person reading this gathering of youthful memories will need a crystal ball to realise that this little chap was going to be very well documented in the files of stupidity held by the police. In fact I became very well known in Steelhouse Lane Police Station. Most Friday nights the police would knock our mom's door and shout up at the bedroom windows 'We've got him again Lucy'. Mom would should back 'Well keep the bastard 'till Monday. I'll know where he is then.' After cooling my heels in the slammer for two days, mom would turn up with the rent book to bail me out. Fined a pound for being drunk and disorderly. The charges got more serious as time went by.

I went back to the scrap iron car-breaking business and did all the things that you leave out of your confession on Sunday morning. A couple of malicious woundings, and one charge of GBH brought prison even closer. I was never a vicious boy - it's just that when the bother started I just got double stuck in, and went ape shit.

We were never bullies and always our trouble was with the boys like us. We would fight some very useful kiddies and I've had just as many tankings as I've dished out. I was forever bringing trouble to the house, and, like most lads, I realised that I had to grow up. Eventually I got a job as a pipe lagger for 'Bernard Hasties Insulation'. They were a Welsh firm with an office in Green Lane, Birmingham. The job meant I would be travelling and working out of town on power stations, buildings sites, sugar beet factories, hospitals, cement works and the like. I soon found the learning fields where proper tough men toiled. I worked hand in hand with iron fighters, pipe fitters, roofers and boilermen. I immediately liked these fellows. They are a hard lot, but too tough to fight over nothing. I always found that they would rather drink and have fun in their leisure hours. Mind you, if bother comes their way they can settle down to it in a most deliberate and effective manner.

I got to be popular with the lads on the sites of labour. In our times of relaxation I would get up to sing at the drop of a hat, my party piece being Bobby Darin's 'Dream Lover' and, though I say it myself, my rendition of this classic ditty was more than just a little turn.

I learned the art of distraction in performance at a very early stage in my life. Because of my status as site worker my usual attire on our lunchtime excursions to the local pubs would be jeans with rolled down wellingtons. When requested to sing, accompanied by a pub pianist unknown to me lighted cigarette ends were flicked with astonishing accuracy down the legs of my mud-covered wellies. Half way through my performance billows of smoke from smouldering socks would occasion a barrage of beer cast in the direction of my endangered undercarriage. In spite of the good natured banter of laughing friends, I always managed finish my song. Surely the mark of a youthful optimist destined to become an unshakeable professional.

Looking back, I suppose the first signs of my future desires to perform were beginning to emerge from deep, hidden fantasies and impossible dreams. Even though I've always immensely loved to sing, not having a theatrical background or any musical knowledge, these were only the fleeting thoughts of a working lad whose mind drifted into the mist of 'if only I could be' musing. The bang of a hammer or the ear shattering demand of Billy Wells (our foreman) often cut through the daydream to remind me that Bradford Street gasworks in Manchester were expecting to be operating this new plant before Christmas.

Amid the daydreams and the leisure I became a very accomplished sheetmetal worker and boiler insulator. My efforts in this trade of migrant workers are visible to this day in places like Bury St Edmonds Hospital, Kidderminster and Newark sugar beet factories, steelworks all over the country, gas works, oil refineries in England, Scotland and Wales. Every power station in our land has pop rivet somewhere snapped in by this minstrel in between reality and imagination. Included in my accomplishments in my thermal insulation engineering days is my contribution to the aluminium covering of the first stainless steel atomic reactor at Winscale nuclear power station.

Whenever we pass by these places on our travels in music, I spin a silent thought of the passed days of hard work and joy I've spent with my workmates. I wonder still how they are getting along. I love to spend time with the grafters near my home and I can listen for hours as they discuss the way in which they have recently rigged a certain job, and conquered a certain problem with their ingenuity and experience. Because of my past life I can understand and follow the gist of their conversations. Sometimes I can even join in with the discussion, relating to them a single problem I have had at a certain time in my former capacity as an engineer. I still enjoy manual work even though my staying power isn't what it was. Arthritis has a tendency to object to swinging a twenty-eight pound sledgehammer on a cold day (or a hot day for that matter).

My first professional engagement (that is, when I got paid for singing) was at the age of eight. The occasion was the Dunlop factory Christmas party. This annual 'do' was held for all of the workers' children. Jelly and all the trimmings, with a Christmas gift for all at the end.

During the proceedings the clown was late so, daringly, the Master of Ceremonies requested contributions from the kids. With my boots blacked I was the first to stick my hand up. To the accompaniment of an out-of-tune upright poorly played piano, I sang 'Gilly-gilly-osemphepher-castonelan-bogan-by-sea', a most endearing little ditty which occasioned every young future Status Quo audience to burst into ear-splitting, head banging backing vocals. I was paid sixpence. My present was a football annual. A most rewarding venture indeed.

The theatrical bug didn't bite that night, but I was well received. However the PA system left a lot to be desired. Even then I wanted to be louder than anyone else!

In between insulating jobs I dabbled in felt-roofing and anything that would take me out of town. I loved being away. It was the adventure of different streets, the accents of hardworking strangers filled my heart with romance. I became an explorer of my own thoughts. I dreamed with my head on the pillows of distant lovers and found comfort in the warm embrace of all the world. I shall move around a bit, I'm sure of that. Anyway, what's a day without

movement? Movement will find the day and the day shall find us love.
'Very nice'.

Chapter nineteen

LOUISE

Strange is the feeling when echoes are calling
I dwell in the morning with time slipping by
With only a question I wait for an answer
Your snow covered picture in words of a song
I see in the distance a time to remember
I carry the moment with birds on the wing
You cast away shadows with light on the mountains
Many's the song I shall sing
So never ending I tell them our story
Of gold and of Gypsies, dragons and kings
Like a soldier of fortune I follow your footsteps
Now brokenhearted I dance on the wind
Now as I tiptoe by you who are sleeping
The scent of the roses lies gently on air
Gone from tomorrow your heart everlasting
Many's the song lying there
Hey, our Louise, here's a song to remember
And if you can come and sing it to me
Hey, our Lousie, sing from May till September
And all through the winter your love shines on me
The baby has grown now, and doing fine
   See Ya!x

Chapter twenty

BILLY JO SPEARS' TOUR

Mervyn Conn rang me to let me know of the forthcoming Billy Jo Spears' tour of Great Britain, and how would I feel about supporting it. Well, I have to tell you I jumped at the chance. I told you earlier about meeting her in Nashville at the mixing sessions of '57 Chevrolet'. Also on the tour would be Paul Richey. Paul is Tammy Wynette's brother-in-law and although he is a great singer and songwriter, I think it's fair to say he is better known in our business as a song publisher, with such songs to his credit as 'Blanket on the Ground' and the Kenny Rogers' classic 'A Fine Time To Leave Me Lucille'.

From Left to Right, Paul Richey, Tony Erdman, Billy-Jo, Frog.

By now I was beginning to gather quite a following on the British scene, so all in all it looked as if this line-up could be a very well attended string of performances. On top of the attractive compliment to me, was the fact that my good friend Tony Erdman was to be the tour manager. Tony is of gigantic stature and a West German Olympic Gold Medal winner for the fine art of proper wrestling. A most dangerous individual in times of unfortunate fracas, but a lightning finisher of such if some unfortunate, unthinking soul should confront him with the slightest possibility that might result in embarrassment to anyone in his charge. Tony is the premier minder to such stars as Frank Sinatra, Michael Jackson and from time to time, members of our Royal Family. If I paint the picture of the uncontrollable beast, let me correct it and tell you that Tony is the epitome of the finest gentleman of high intelligence and academic achievement and, I might add, a very good friend of mine (thank God).

It was necessary for our band to accompany Paul Richey in his performance and, to their eternal credit, can I say that they did a superb job for the man.

After the rehearsals for timing and lighting plot creation BJ arrived from America. We all congregated at the Tara Hotel in Bayswater, London. After three days' discussion and introduction our show was ready for the road. I had reminded BJ of our meeting in Nashville, but, sadly, she didn't remember it. I felt a bit of a prat, but I soon got over the embarrassment because she is such a nice person. I remember our American producer Larry Butler telling me that Billy Jo was his favourite lady. It's not difficult to believe that, because it was soon obvious to me that she is the most professional of artistes with a superb voice and style. Her performance as far as I could see is both genuine and sincere. As a singer and lady she is second to none. A true First Lady of Country music. Good on you gal.

As usual, my job was to open the show - a twenty minute performance - but then introduce my good friend Paul Richey. Paul looks like a film star, six foot three inches tall, dead good looking and a deep voice of classic American southern quality. My introduction went something like this: 'Ladies and Gentlemen, I have a very privileged opportunity now to introduce you to an American artiste of great talent. He's very tall, extremely handsome, a great songwriter with a superb voice - and I hate him' (the audience would laugh), please make welcome Mr Paul Richey'.

Paul loved my introduction to him and we became, and still are, great friends.

Billy Jo Spears' guitar player was a lay preacher, and every Sunday we were on the road he would hold a service for us. His nickname was the 'Rev'. I always found his sermons quite beautifully delivered and sometimes thought-provoking.

I remember Tony Erdman saying to me that before the tour was over he was going to get saved even if it killed him. We would celebrate the weekly failure of this ambition with a small libation in the Sunday lunchtime hotel bar. I would say, 'Don't worry Tony. If God ever needs taking care of there's not a better man he could have in heaven'. 'I take your point my dear fellow. Perhaps I'll get saved next week'. With this comment my big pal ordered another two large libations, a small hiccup in the search for a pure heart.

Although I've always enjoyed my inclusion in these tours it has been my ambition to see how we would get on heading our own tour. Everything in this business is alive and moving and no one has the time to wait for something to happen to them. Anyone can be busy moaning about the way they are not getting the breaks; but while you're complaining the best chance of your life will flash by and you won't even notice. All of my time on these American tours was spent getting to know the theatre people and finding out how you go about financing and planning your effort. I have to tell all of my peers that promotion is not a simple affair. I had to make sure that we made a good professional impression, not only with the theatre audiences, but with the people who work within the theatre world. All of them are indifferent to the type of show you are likely to promote, but they do like your offering and your temperament to be of a professional nature. To wait for a big promoter to do it for you is folly, because promoting is a risky business. The first thing he will look for is how much the artiste is likely to cost and how big a draw is he or she. His first absolute outlay is the artistes. Once he contracts them he is totally committed to paying them. He will never be wanting to look for the box office takings in order to pay them. He has to be able to afford to lose.

In my case in self promotion, all I had to do was pay us. So if we lost we were hardly likely to sue ourselves. It just meant going without for a week. Because I had made a good impression with the theatre managers some of them were prepared to do a percentage deal of 70-30, thus saving us the expense of up-front theatre hire costs.

First of all I had to be sure that our theatres would not be empty. Not just for the financial loss, but for the sheer embarrassment of empty houses.

The theatre world is very small and bad news travels fast. Bad houses can set you back quite a bit when you're working on a percentage deal.

First though we must finish our tour with Billy Jo Spears. It was a fantastic show to be involved with. We also had the added beauty of our own fans among the audience.

Chapter twenty one

ROMSLEY HILL

So here I had an idea - to do what I hoped would put British Country music on a higher level.

We all know that whatever plans we make have a habit of twisting and turning, and none of us can be sure that anything we try will work out.

Like many of us, I've just followed the pattern of life, treading water and hoping that tomorrow will be better than today. When we are young it's easy to get over disappointment, and it's true that people don't laugh at a young person's failures. As we grow, however, the generous love given (quite rightly) to a youngster's efforts fades away somewhat with the passing of years. There will always be people who want you to fail, but the joyful incentive to an older trier is to prove them wrong.

Someone in Country music once said to me, there are no superstars in British Country music. I disagree. There are hundreds of them. I say to him, don't judge an artiste by his lack of a cadillac or his empty pockets. There has been many a genius (American and British) who never had a chance to shine on the label of luck. Have no doubt about it, there's many a great heart beating under a ragged coat. No superstars in British Country? Don't you believe it. There you are, my dears, starry eyed and laughin'. I can see you and so can thousands of others. They watch and listen every day. They, and I, think you are simply great. Keep going!

I'm a fighter, so I'll only fail if the fans don't want me or God decides to lay me low for a while. That has happened to me and many others before. Just when you're ready to live a little you get hurt.

I had felt strange for a while, but you know how it is when you're young. 'This will soon pass'. The trouble is that serious illness sneaks up on you when you're not looking. It arrives without invitation. It will not ring the doorbell; nor will it lie to you, or stand in your vision so that you can judge it's appearance or reason for being there. Unlike a burglar, it will not simply enter through a secluded window and steal to make the fine, precious gatherings of your world his. It will not rummage through the memories and knick-knacks of your labour and select what it fancies. It will not break and scatter the things that have no value to it.

Illness has no fence to take it's plunder to. It has no sense of consequence and it is indifferent to a way of escape. It will by-pass every alarm system in your body, find your soul, and make a home there. Only when it is good and ready it will bite. The first knowledge of its presence won't alert you to danger. Your visitor will knock the door from the inside just to let you know that it's arrived. Its only reason for being there is to kill you. How strong you are, or it is, will determine whether or not it will succeed.

For the second time in my young life I was in conflict tuberculosis. In the next few years I was to learn a lot about this lethal companion. Even though I had made its acquaintance before, I had been too young to understand the beating it gave me. I was four years old, and got the bus to hospital. Mom came home without me.

It was not the illness that took me by the ears and shook me. It was the isolation because of the contagious nature of my kidnapper.

The place I was taken to had no pictures of Mickey Mouse and Bambi on the walls. There were no rainbows on the windows, or strings with bright things hanging from the ceilings. The beds were made of black painted iron, and I was frightened. Even at my very young age I somehow knew that our mom would not be coming to take me home tomorrow.

I was under school age and too confused to be objectionable. I just wanted to walk away from it. Not with anyone in particular but just to go through any door no matter where it might lead me. I was immediately harnessed to the bed with canvas belts. This had such an effect on me that I remember to this very day the emptiness of my isolation.

You see isolation and bed rest was the only treatment for TB in those days. Somewhere in the world there were scientific research pioneers of a medical nature looking for streptomycin. One day they found it and many years later they saved my life, along with millions of others.

I spent my early growing years in the Yardley Sanatorium for Contagious Diseases. I learned to grow up without love. It was too dangerous to hug and kiss anyone of us.

Special times like Christmas or Easter, birthdays and the seaside and no meaning to me. I learned to live each day without the hope of ever going home. I became indifferent to human touch. I didn't know what going to the pictures was, or being asked to do something. I was told, and learned to obey.

After three years I was told I would be going home and, God forgive me, I didn't know what they meant.

I left Yardley Sanatorium holding the hand of my mother, just as I had entered it. Now we were accompanied by a man dressed in a brown pin striped suit. He was Bill Bland, my new dad. I was to grow up to bury him in an air of unfortunate family indifferences. Because of life's circumstances he had drifted away from us; but he was the father of my four treasured brothers. Before he died I thanked him for them. We were alone on a Saturday morning as he passed away. He smiled at me and called me 'son'.

It was the silent thoughts of a little boy that said goodbye to the world I had got to know. The pretty girl who had become my friend had also gone home. She got better before I did. As she had progressed from her illness she was moved to another area of the Sanatorium to a less contagious ward.

One morning it had been snowing and, as always, our beds were moved on to a long verandah. The huge doors were opened and we would lie there all day. This was considered to be beneficial to our recovery. I had discovered where my friend had been taken and innocently I brought some snow in and put it on her bed so she could play in it. Once again I was hurriedly harnessed to my bed. My first present to a young lady had fallen on stony ground. I never saw her again. Her name was Emma, and in our unintentional childlike way, we had helped each other to cope with our loneliness. Although I have been loved as much as anyone by my family, I have never truly felt at home anywhere in the world ever since.

During my many private conversations with our mother I told her that, and, as always, she understood perfectly. She had had too many children for her not to know each one of us personally. There was nothing anyone of us could feel, or do, that could trick or surprise here. One of us thought he could, but he will have to take that nonsense to the grave with him.

The first time round I didn't know I was ill. I simply thought I was being abandoned. I had no idea of the danger I was in. This time, however, I knew about fitness and health. I was a strong young man in almost unbearable pain. Like all of us, I kept it a secret for over a year, but it soon became obvious to my friends that something was wrong. I began to find it difficult to do my job and became indifferent to youthful fun.

I was working at the Blue Circle Cement Works in Westbury, Wiltshire. I finally bucked up courage to confess my dilemma to my close workmate Jack Evans. He had noticed the change in me, and convinced me to go to hospital. I had a X-ray and blood test at the Westbury Cottage Hospital. The results were sent to my own doctor and my manual working life was over.

I became one of the thousands of people who spend their entire confused thoughts in anticipation of their next appointment. It became quite clear very quickly that I was very seriously ill. I was beginning to lose spirit, and something was killing me.

I was assigned to the care of a young Irishman, Dr Austin. He in turn introduced my case to a renal specialist surgeon, Mr Henderson. After the many painful tests I was summoned to Mr Henderson's surgery, where Dr Austin informed me that I was dying from tuberculosis of the kidneys. I learned that pulmonary tuberculosis (that is to say tuberculosis of the lungs) can later return to other parts of the body.

It's rare, but it does happen. This type of TB is not contagious but it is lethal. Mr Henderson gave me (without immediate treatment) a month or two to live. I had to go away again.

I asked Mr Henderson to hide the seriousness of my illness from my family. They have never mentioned it to me, so I presume he kept his promise.

No one person on earth can fight serious illness alone. I was to find an army of people prepared to sacrifice their every hour, and use every skill, care and concern in order to save my life.

It's no one's fault when you become ill - it's the luck of the draw. I've been around hundreds of sick and dying men, women and children most of my life. I've witnessed such courage in the face of death that would humble he biggest moaner ever born. My brother-in-law Arthur Dyer, drove me to the hospital - Romsley Hill Sanatorium - nestled in the Clent Hills. It was a difficult journey for him. We have always been great friends. I had worked with him at 'Nock's Brickyard', running the machine barrows - as fit as a fiddle. To take me, weak and dying, to this place made him very sad indeed.

We hardly spoke on the way there. It was a beautiful morning and on our arrival I just walked for about an hour. I really didn't want to go in. I imagined, deep down, that I would never come out. Patiently Arthur walked with me, not saying a single word. There were rhododendron bushes all over the place, beautiful lawns, flower beds and hundreds of house-martins chattering, getting through their day. I remember thinking that they could leave any time they wanted. but until the coming of winter this was their home.

The hospital was an old manor house converted into wards of four to five beds; but for its purpose, it was a very lovely place to be.

I decided to check in and Arthur followed me. The reception area was like a small Scottish hotel. A kindly welcoming face greeted us. 'We've been expecting you Mr Froggatt. You're late'. 'I'm sorry. We got caught in the traffic', I lied. 'Unusual for a Sunday' she replied. 'Never mind. You're here now. Too late for lunch I'm afraid'. (As if I could have eaten anything anyway.) The dear lady rang a bell. Not an official sounding device but more of a comforting rural buzz. This occasioned the arrival of yet another Irishman, small in stature, with dyed black hair. The heavy horn rimmed glasses perched on the end of his nose gave him a very friendly, strangely comic look. I immediately liked him.

In his broad Southern Irish brogue he introduced himself. 'Now of all titles of Irishmen born, me name's Pat, and yourself, Raymond, no doubt' (he smiled reassuringly). 'I'll take you to your ward. You'll change, give your clothes to your man and I'll bring you a cup of tea. Now how's that for a bargain?' We followed him along a corridor and up a winding 'Agatha Christie' type staircase. Pat talked all the way. 'Other services I offer are the fetching of newspapers, the putting on of bets, even the occasional tip if your goodself be undecided as to which horse you'll be after losing your money on'. We turned into a short corridor with a dead end. I was almost there.

My heart sank. Arthur would be gone soon. I wouldn't be seeing anyone I knew until the following Wednesday. Visiting was twice a week - Wednesday afternoon and Sunday afternoon.

I changed my clothes, got into bed and had a cup of tea with Arthur. He didn't know how to leave, and I didn't want him to go. 'Well Thanks Cake (Cake is his nickname). You'd better get going. They'll be worrying at home.' 'See you, Ray, I'll bring mom and Jean over on Wednesday'. 'OK mate. Mind how you go'. The small sliding door shut and Arthur was gone.

I looked around at the five other beds in the small ward, acknowledged the occupants with a youthful shy nod, and pretended to read a book I was totally lost.

In the routine of long-stay sanatoriums the feeling of strangeness soon leaves you. We were all on the same treatment of streptomycin and foul tasking pasana medicine. Consequently we had much in common to talk about.

There's no doubt about it, there is a lot of time to kill in long-stay hospitals and so the occupational therapists are of paramount importance Many of the fellows didn't bother with the various pastimes offered. Some of the chaps were allowed to walk in the grounds and find pleasure in conversation with people from other parts of the hospital. I wasn't allowed out of my ward for the first six months, so I made plenty of bunny rabbits teddy bears, table lamps, tiger toys, elephants, leather briefcases, wallets and wooden ships. When these efforts were taken from the hospital by members of my family they would have to be sterilised and sealed in cellophane bags. I felt like a leper.

There were times when I was in so much pain I almost gave up the fight. As always, the nurses would recognise the signs of pending defeat and take your battered spirit to their own hearts and love you out of your despair. They don't learn that at a training course, it's just inborn, natural love that springs mightily from the souls of extraordinary young girls and mature women. We in Great Britain have the finest people in the world to take care of us. When we are struck low by illness they will fight until the battle is won. If you are lost they will privately break their hearts, dry their tears and start all over again. For them there is another broken life to mend. Always another life.

My bed was by an old-fashioned sash window with small square panes of glass. From there I could see the rolling Clent hills, a distant road, and the occasional flash of colour as cars went by. Who was in that? Where were they going? Someone from a window is watching. Someone from a window is dreaming. Someone from a window is getting well and getting stronger. I was going to make it.

Sixty miles away a young boy was leaving school. Very soon we will meet for the first time. His name is H. Cain.

It became clear to Dr Austin that although the tuberculosis was beaten they had failed to save the left kidney. It had finally died, and had to be removed. I didn't consider this to be bad news. In fact, to me, it was good news. It meant that the fight was almost over. Once I had got through that episode I would be well again. Not the boy I was, not the boxer or the brainless youth, the brickyard worker, pipe lagger or sheetmetal worker. Perhaps I could be a singer. Who knows?

During my time at Romsley Hill I had watched the house martins come and go three times. I had seen the snow cover the beautiful grounds. I had seen boys come to this place and never go home; lost to the invisible killer that with a whim or fancy will attack everyone of us. Young Simon, whose heels permanently touch the back of his head because of spinal TB, doomed to lie on his side for his entire life, and yet smiling still. I have seen the empty look behind the eyes of shell-shocked parents who are completely floored by the damage that this disease is capable of inflicting.

My existence and directions have altered immeasurably. Basically, I have become afraid of people's company. I had to deal with childhood isolation with a mind that was too young to understand. I had to mark time in the face of imminent death, with the heart of an immature youth. Sadly I have become used to being alone and I find myself comfortable with shadows. The light of the world intrigues me and I truly love the people who dance on it. I like to be part of their days and, in many ways, I am. God gave me the arms and lips of words, so I am able to hug and kiss the whole world with songs. People return my poetic advances with the compliment of applause and from my stage of tears I am fulfilled.

I left Romsley Hill in an ambulance, heading towards Dudley Road Hospital. Here the final tests were to take place before the last round of the battle for life. A little time at home (as I've mentioned earlier) and then back to the familiar walls of fear.

Mr Henderson was quite frank in is his pre-op discussion with me. We had got to know each other well enough over the years, and pussyfooting around was not on, for either of us. 'We know, Raymond, that we are going to find a dead kidney in there, and we are going to remove it.' He paused a short time. 'On the other hand we can't be sure of any other problems we might find, and to what extent other damage, if any, may have been done by the tuberculosis. It isn't going to be easy, but you're the stubbornest little bugger I have ever know, and so am I'. He smiled and continued; 'so between us we are one hell of a man to take on this problem. You are as strong as we can get you now, so we will do our bit, and the rest is up to you.'

The job was over and done. It just remained that for 365 days a year, for three years, I was to have an injection of stretemyen in my backside - a most disagreeable start to the day, but I am alive.

For over thirty years I have had my yearly visit to Dr Austin's surgery in Birmingham for my annual X-rays and blood tests. Dr Austin and I have watched each other grow old; me from an endangered youth and he to an almost-retiring aged hospital doctor.

On my most recent visit he told me that Romsley Hill Sanatorium had been closed down and turned into luxury apartments. Gone are the sad faces at the windows, no more tears of joy and oft-times despair. Gladys's tea trolley that squeaked and rolled around the corridors telling the time of day to people who couldn't have cared less for clocks, has served its final purpose. So where is Pat? Still betting the horses? Young Simon walks now with Jesus and laughs in paradise.

The house martins still return, and instead of the torn-off ragged edges of a family, they will hear the normal doings of happy homes, the shouts and squeals of playing children and the warm breeze of ordinary, ordered life.

If there could be a memorial day for the people who fought the battle of tuberculosis there would be oceans of poppies for the casualties. The medals of honour would be a hundred thousandfold, awarded to the fearless army of doctors and nurses who saved so many. I am a survivor of that episode in human tragedy. I arrived there broken and weak. I came from there strong and grown, with a mind made mature by the courage and passing of people coloured more golden that I could ever be.

From Yardley Sanatorium and Romsley Hill, I came to work on the stage at the London Palladium. My songs contain the echoes of everyone I have ever known, and the music shall contain the whispers of a secret story that has no meaning and, thus far, has never been told.

Rob Zuradzki had left Mervyn Conn's employ. With him he took his idea for a 'Best of British' tour. The famous promoter Derek Block gave the use of one of his offices for the purpose of organising the construction of this project.

My tour with Billy Jo Spears was complete so I was free, at Rob's request, for me to headline it. This was a great opportunity for me to measure whether or not we had any drawing power as an all-British show.

Rob decided that the line-up should run as follows. Rosemarie (the dear girl!). My good friend and drinking partner, Kelvin Henderson, a man of monumental capacity and a brewer of such strange concoctions that the annual wine taster's convention of Bordeaux would have become a gathering of gibbering idiots at a fire-breathing contest! A most talented chap indeed and a most endearing companion of fun. Another band of talented minstrels were to grace the stage on this venture - Yellowstone Picnic Band. With yours truly, we had a show. From my point of view it was a great experiment.

Individually all of us artistes on the show had our own fans, but would they come to a theatre to see us? After all, they had been used to seeing us in a club environment.

This wasn't an expensive promotion. There were no hotels provided for us, or tour bus. The PA system was provided by my outfit. I don't know what the other artistes were paid but we got two hundred and fifty pounds a show between five musicians. Also out of that we had to pay our own crew, our own hotel bills and general road expenses.

The promoter's outlay, apart from the meagre artiste's fees, were expensive advertising, theatre hire costs and the compere's fees. If this tour had not worked there was a loss to incur so, fair play to Derek and Rob, they took the chance.

As it turned out, I believe the tour made a net profit of fourteen thousand pounds. To someone like Derek Block this isn't a great venture. Although he had made a profit it wasn't enough for him to go overboard with enthusiasm to repeat the enterprise. However, it gave me the knowledge I needed to find that the people would come to see us in theatres. For self-promotion I now had the experience, the know-how, the contacts, and most important of all, the fans.

All I needed now was the courage to fail and the fans the help me show sceptics that we, the British artistes, are all right. For years now I have been honoured with the BMCA Artiste of the Year Award. I receive it with gratitude on behalf of us all.

Chapter
twenty two

THE WARSAW PACT

Mervyn Conn had a telephone call out of the blue from 'Pagart', the Ministry of Music in Poland. The Polish people informed him of a Music Festival to be held in M'Rongowa to celebrate the lifting of marshal law in their unfortunate, beautiful country. Would it be possible for the

Ministry to book George Hamilton IV to star at this week-long holiday of joy and (for the Polish people) freedom, of a sort.

The festival was only three weeks away from its opening day and Mervyn had to inform them that George would be in Canada touring for two months. When asked if he could suggest another artiste my name came to mind. Although our business relationship had ended Mervyn knew that I would not disgrace his recommendation of me.

There were strange laws to abide by in this occupied country and one of them was that I would only be allowed to take two members of my band with me. It was clear to me that H. Cain and Phil Capaldi (my drummer at that time) would be the obvious choices to accompany me on this venture. The rest of my musicians were to be made up from Polish musicians. They would be unfamiliar with our way of playing, so H. Cain would be most valuable in his leadership of our Polish friends and anyone who has worked in a band will know that a drummer who knows how the rhythm and tempos sit will be a great time saver in rehearsal.

The deal was this: we would be supplied with our return flight tickets to and from Warsaw and our transport from Warsaw to M'Romgowa would be by taxi supplied by the Ministry. We would be supplied with as many Zloty (Polish currency) as we needed. This money could be spent on anything we needed whilst we were inside Poland. The money would not be allowed out of the country and we were forbidden to bring anything we had bought with it, home. So these monies were very generous internal expenses. Our fee for our contribution was to be made in American dollars and given to us with a release document on our departure at the airport. The fee was 150 dollars - about 75 pounds sterling. Not over payment you might think, but we have to remember that Poland at that time was under the occupation of the Soviet Army.

It's very difficult for our people to understand what effect occupation can mean to a nation. Fortunately, our fathers, mothers and grandparents have always been able to fight off our would-be aggressors and with their courage and lives have preserved our freedom.

None of us owe anything to any of our governments, or indeed to any one man or woman. Conflict between nations, to my mind, is the result of politicians operating at their very worst, and should never be glorified in the result of our victory. You and I walk in freedom because of the blood so unselfishly spilt by our neighbours all over our nation.

I have witnessed first hand the dire straits our Polish cousins suffer because of the geographical position of their unfortunate country. They have been raided, plundered, raped and mercilessly humiliated for centuries, and yet to find a more courageous nation of hope and vision would be impossible. As blades of grass stepped on by all manner of boot, they spring to life constantly and from crushed beauty they bloom again and again, and again.

Our interpreter had an unpronounceable name, but kindly asked us to call him Walter. After a rigourous Custom's check we were on our way to M'Rongowa, a three hour drive from Warsaw.

The festival was held in a huge clearing at the centre of a pine forest. The site was an amphitheatre-style slope, with the rear of the huge stage backing on to the shores of a lake, milling and buzzing with the excited sound of over 50,000 people.

The event was to be televised nationally, live, throughout the final day of this incredibly well organised event. There were bands from Holland, Yugoslavia, Hungary, Czechoslovakia and Poland. We were here to headline the final moments and, like many time before, no one had ever heard of us.

We had been in M'Rongowa for two days before we had to play in order to rehearse with our Polish musicians. With the help of out interpreter, Walter, and the natural marriage of music makers the whole world over, we soon had a show. The KGB man who accompanied us everywhere, vetted all of the lyrics I had decided to sing. He agreed to them all except 'Teach Me, Pa'. Apparently he felt the song was subversive (God and he only know why).

We joined in the festivities for two days and what a great people the Poles are. So much love in their faces. These same faces that hid the pain of their existence under the occupation of the Soviet forces. The lack of ordinary things, so absent from their lives that bright silver treasure of simple wants are as distant as stars. The fall of disappointment, so fierce, soaks them to the bone. The great wall of indifference surrounds their every day and the chain of cruelty keeps them within an arm's reach of freedom. I was to entertain these magnificent people and the thought of that humbled me beyond belief. My God, I prayed I could.

While H. and Phil rehearsed I asked Walter to teach me a Polish folk song. He taught me, and I learned parrot fashion the words and tune to the most famous Polish song in history. It is called 'Shva-ja-veshka'. The amount of vodka I drank ensured that my Polish accent was perfect. Walter told me 'Froggie, if you sing that they will go ape-shit'.

The time came for me to perform. My introduction was in the Polish language with an attempt at my name 'Remon Frowgard' from Great Britain. The people stood and cheered and I sang the only Polish song I knew. Walter was right - they went ape-shit! I was home and dry.

I walked among the audience with a radio microphone and sang to my new friends. Every song was welcomed with great ovation. A compliment indeed. Even our KGB man tapped his foot and clapped his hands to my simple song 'Roly'.

Because of the television coverage I became an instant success all over Poland with hundreds of people at Warsaw airport to wave us goodbye. I have been there on one occasion since. I find now that the people wave the Union Jack with their own emblem, side by side, in honour of our country. 'Jen cu jer Polska'. I will see you again.

For two years now it has been impossible for us to visit them, with the gradual anti Communist revolution in eastern Europe. I have been invited once again in the light of different circumstances throughout their land. As you are reading this book I will have been, and come home. I took with me the blessings of every British Country music fan and I have wished them well from us all.

As the plane left Warsaw I could see in the distance the waving souls, who were not allowed to leave. Walter told me how privileged the people felt that others would arrive to entertain them, and how they felt less forgotten in their isolation to hear different voices from a world outside. I've seen the monuments erected in honour of a hundred miners that were shot and killed for going on strike. I've witnessed lines of people over a mile long, just because sardines were on sale. The expressions on the faces of Polish musicians at the sight of a tube of toothpaste (impossible to get in Poland) were those of children on birthdays. Beneath their tortured spirit lies a smouldering defiance that one day will blossom and become once again the free talented people they will always be.

Chapter twenty three

THOSE I DEPEND ON

So, then, as I think about it all I find in every corner blue and gold. There is joy and sadness beneath all shelter, that leaves me breathless in open air. There is only love, with a million arms reaching out to guide us all. Light so distant and dim, yet waiting the weary still. I shall ever run to touch the hand that seeks to catch my heart. I know that I shall hold for ever the fleeting moments of laughing eyes. These eyes of people I have never met have sparkled because of songs. I can only deliver these offerings in the best way I know how. Music comes from somewhere inside of me and I am as mystified as anyone else as to their origin. They are caught in mid air by some people, and as easily dismissed by others. That is the way of all artistic creation. Success and failure run hand in hand and, to my mind, should never be labelled good and bad.

A national Country presenter once asked me what I thought the reason was that I had so much success in the business and why was it that so many people loved my songs. I'm bound to say that in fifty years of life I had never felt so insulted. His question was unanswerable and it implied that he felt at a loss to understand why anyone should be entertained by my presence in this business. I don't think that Frank Sinatra or Elvis Presley could answer that and I doubt whether this fellow would have had the audacity to ask them.

I have never been astonished or mystified by anyone's success in this business. It's the constant surprise of what we witness that makes the whole thing so interesting. We all, of course, have our particular favourite artiste, but certainly that can never mean that everything else is rubbish. To imply that, is to insult everybody else's opinion.

I have known many tough people in my life in every area of poverty and privilege there is. I have seen heroism in every avenue of existence. I, like many, have been a victim of cowardly abuse of trust and unadulterated lies, delivered with such contempt that it's difficult to drive home the nail of forgiveness into the cross of human nature. I look around my days and nights among the clouds and sun, to find all manner of great people. They drift and sway within the sight of God, while dealing with tragedy and love all the same.

My heart is as defenceless as yours against the brutal indifference of life's beatings. My comfort waits in the misty rooms where, beyond a light, people sit and, for a song, they throw me love. Though sometimes, with my spirit crushed, I smile and sing. As they catch the song, so I catch their love and take it home with me.

I salute my fellow British Country artistes because I know their days. I am aware of their pain and I marvel at their courage. We share the same stages and chase the same dream. Our efforts are in the hands of our critics and our future in the hands of our fans.

If you are looking for toughness, you will find it in every bus and van on any road that leads to a venue large or small. They know who they are and where on the ladder they stand. Their commitment to their art is gigantic, and long may they live. That is the only answer to this question I know. That is why we succeed and that is why people love our songs. If you can't see that and you won't help us, then leave us alone.

The way I see it nothing great comes from wealth. Every masterpiece of art was born on poverty. Every discovery of a scientific nature was relentlessly pursued on the flimsy shoestring of donations from the common people. The great modern day aid programmes are praised with an ocean of monies that came from the pockets of hard-working people. Every artiste I have ever known came from humble beginnings. So the company I keep is fine by me. I will never have to ask them why they think people love them. I already know.

I took on this life because I wanted to write and sing and I'm damned if I'm ever going to apologise for being British to anyone. I have told you of the people who have done me the honour of working with me and it's certainly true that without them I have no way of performing. The musicians have been many, but all of them important to my day.

The great fun I've had working with Phil Capaldi (who now plays drums for Joe Brown) were some of the most memorable times of my life. His magic humour and infectious energy are unforgettable. His warm friendship is an anchor in anyone's life. Dave Nilo, a great bassist and quite one of the nicest human beings I have ever known (Dave now plays bass for Mike D'Abo of Manfred Mann fame). David Bailey, a superb keyboard player and songwriter (now with Sarahjory). My work has been complimented by the wonderfully talented John Casswell (now with Lynsey St John), Phil Lyons and Mal Morris, two great bass players.

Being in a band together doesn't always work as any musician will tell you. Some things suit some players and others just fancy a change. It's understandable to us all, but their contribution to the whole thing remains (in this piece of our time) fully appreciated, and I thank them.

My band at this time is blessed with the talents of the irrepressible Roger Browne, a Birmingham musician of 'once seen never to be forgotten' qualities. Roger has been playing for years, always heading his own bands. I've known Roger since we were babies and, although I have always admired his musicianship, I honestly didn't think that he would ever play in our band.

Roger's outfits have always been (although melodic) rather on the undisciplined, noisy side. His band, The Symbolics, were filling places all over the Midlands for years. He then started a band called 'Gerry and the Atrics', due to his musicians rapidly deteriorating into the autumn of their years.

Anyone who knows Roger will agree that he is a superbly accomplished musician and a man of unfailing loyalty. He is a tremendously memorable person, with a wit of immeasurable joy. I am truly honoured to work with him.

The difference in all people never ceases to trigger the interest in me. In contrast to Roger we boast one of the most reserved people in our tremendous drummer, Tom Farnell. Tom is a man of staggering experience and quite definitely one of the finest musicians anyone will ever hear,

because he has spent a lifetime in this business, there is very little anyone could teach him in the art of surviving on the road. As I've mentioned reservedness let me say right away that Tom can get his rocks off with the best of them. If the brandy is flowing and the cracks looking promising you've got yourself one hell of a party person. He is positively crackers, with a singing voice that will demolish walls. Many is the time when you wish they would burst his pretty balloon and take his moon away just so you can get some sleep! A fine man, and he is one of my treasured human beings.

Bruce Caulkin is our bass player now and also a man of great experience. He fitted into our outfit without any problems. he, like all of the other musicians, has an inborn instinct of compliment to play new music. Although his style is unique to his own measure, he has turned his talent to fit my needs. Both Roger and Bruce are fine lead singers so I am assured of excellent back vocals at all times.

It's difficult for any singer (who naturally sings lead parts) to be beneath the line of projection and thus compliment the piece they are performing. It's very easy to fall into the trap of over-singing. The balance between lead and backing vocals will then be spoilt.

Because of their knowledge and experience Roger and Bruce are able to compromise this problem fully. They are part of my band, and together with Tom, H.C. and me, we make music. The same music we know will not please everyone but with it we remain original and true to our followers.

Raymond Froggatt is like every other entertainer on earth, with a deep desire to capture the hearts of as many people as is humanly possible. This is a foolish desire because, whoever you may be, there will always remain (true the nature of humankind) people who will be indifferent to whatever you produce. If, however, you are in show-business this desire is imperative, for without it you will run out of steam. It is unfortunate that because of this dream we will all be hurt deeply many times. It's part and parcel of this business we take on.

Because of who I am, like many others I am hopelessly vulnerable to unfair jibes and slander. On the other hand, because of who I am, there are thousands of people who take my part. The balance of my life is directed by the people who love me. There isn't any procrastination in my daily commitments. I am aware of all the people I depend on. I consider it my duty to be constantly working, so that I might return some of the security they have so unselfishly built around my life.

People who listen and get enjoyment from my music are irreplaceable. I, like every artiste born, get only my share of a public who are moving in the breeze of other lilting melodies of life. It seems important to me that my efforts are forever flowing so that my shelter can choose from the confusion of rhythm and air, their souls resting place for a moment of peace in the stormy ocean of ordinary days.

I am a common man with the simple needs of a child from the streets. My ambitions are born in me, and I am carried along only as far as the people who love me will allow me to go. My mind is sharpened by the vigour I seen in others and my whole world is heading for a field of roses where to lay down with the echoes of a thousand songs is my destiny.

My temperament will pull me this way and that. My mistakes, always, will be many, but my line of movement will be honest and deliberate.

Although the art of entertaining people is in its own self (providing you have a little talent) a simple, enjoyable affair, the mechanics of the modern-day entertainment industry is very complicated indeed.

If you are trying to do it properly you will need many people to make it work. The whole area of this industry demands professionals, not only in entertaining but also in negotiating your every step.

It's never any good dragging amateur ideas into the world of professionals. They won't even bother to laugh at you. They will simply show you the door. All of us are only as strong as the amount of seats we can fill. I know for certain that there are promoters who work very hard indeed to promote the efforts of British Country music artistes. It is to their eternal credit that I and many other artistes are able to reach the ears of thousands of fans throughout the British Isles. These illustrious people organise against all odds to keep the fantastic country festivals going. None of them have the benefit of wealthy sponsors to help them with the all-important finance to cushion then from the constant looming cloud of the ever present monster - the financial disaster.

The hundreds upon hundreds of small country club promoters who, with their amazing fortitude, keep their weekly gatherings going through thick and thin, sometimes culminating in a Summer Festival - I take my hat off to them. They are priceless individuals. Between them all they have created an admirable scene. Without them, I am just someone who would like to sing a song I cannot play alone.

I have learned over many years that the music industry will only value an artiste for his or her potential on that day. The love of true fans, however, will last always. So many are the days my dears.

Chapter twenty four

WHAT NOT TO DO

People often ask why I no longer drive a car. The answer I give is simple; I'm just no bloody good at driving! The scrapes I've had whilst being in charge of these admirable conveyors of humankind are legendary. The most amazing thing, which is certainly mind-boggling, is that in my entire driving experience to this day I have never had the black mark of an endorsement for any type of misdemeanour.

I am bound to say, however, that my discussions and explanations with puzzled officers of the law are many fold.

The first songwriting success I had was to enable me to succeed the ambition of every youngster born - the ownership of a posh motor. A trip to the motor showrooms and at last the ultimate pose vehicle of my dreams - a Daimler Sovereign saloon. What a car! I drove it all over the place. It had a stereophonic eight track motoroller sound system and the ultimate touch of luxury - a colour television set for the rear passengers.

The first mishap in this fine car was the only one that was genuinely not my fault.

It happened one fine day in Birmingham. Bev Bevan, who was then playing in the Move, invited me to the opening of this new record store. Along with lots of other Birmingham musicians I arrived at the shop, which was positioned near Hall Green in Brum.

I was early, so that all press and other musicians could see my new car. I parked it right outside the main doors and felt youthfully proud of myself as I emerged from this beautiful work of mechanical art. The press photographers took their pictures as I slowly locked the vehicle doors, making sure that they had plenty of time to get me in my full posing stature. I hadn't reached the door when from behind me I heard an almighty crash-bang-wallop. As I turned, the boot of my car was sailing over the bonnet top and two very flash wheel covers were travelling down the street at about sixty miles an hour. One of the rear tyres went immediately flat and the rear door electric window fell out on to the pavement.

Ozzy Osbourne had arrived in his new Mercedes and, from his explanation ('misjudged the speed and stopping distance. Sorry Frog') instead of a picture of me standing by my new status symbol the evening newspaper displayed a photo of mine and Ozzy's cars welded together in a tangle of destruction with me and Ozzy scratching our heads in disbelief. The headline to the picture read 'Mr F's four letter fiasco'. We all had a good laugh and drink and, like all youngsters, we saw the funny side of it. My Daimler was repaired as good as new but I decided to buy a bigger vehicle to run about in. My choice was an American Ranch Wagon estate car. This silver machine was twenty feet long, with a red leather interior and room for nine passengers. Behind the controls of this beast I looked like a small growth attached to the steering wheel!

One evening at the local pub in our village of Henley in Arden I suggested to some of the local lads a late night party at my home. In about three seconds flat the Ranch Wagon was full of girls and fellows in high singing mood. The party was about to begin.

I got to the controls of this magnificent vehicle and slowly pulled away from the kerb in the High Street. My home was about two miles away and it was situated on top of a high bank. The entrance to my home was accessible from a narrow dirt road with a thirty foot drop on the left hand side of the rise. It was pissing down with rain so foolishly I decided to reverse up the slope to save me turning the car round later. Slowly reversing up the dodgy slope it hadn't occurred to me that the thirty foot drop was now on my right hand side. Half way up, the car seemed to drift to the right, occasioning the rear wheels to spin. In the pitch blackness with a howling wind and almost monsoon type rain, I informed my happy singing car load of eager party-goers that I would get out to see what the problem was. I opened the door and promptly disappeared down into the abyss of bushes, small trees and brambles, landing onto the road below. Slightly shocked, battered and soaking wet I gingerly looked up to see the huge heavy motor unbelievably perched half way over the cliff and grotesquely swaying to and fro.

I shouted to my friends (who were completely unaware of the danger) 'Lean to your left'. A bonny face appeared at the window and immediately paled into confused fear as the realisation of their dilemma hit home. I hurried and climbed the very difficult slope and reached my home to ring for assistance.

I knew the local copper at the Henley Police Station so I informed him that we needed help.

Roy said 'Calm down Froggy, now what do you need? Police, Fire or Ambulance?' Feeling at a loss I replied, 'I think I'd better have all three'. After a rough outline of what had occurred Roy decided to come out to take a look for himself. On his arrival Roy stood with his hands on his hips, mouth wide open and shaking his head. 'How the bloody hell have you managed to do this, Frog?' 'I don't know, Roy, it just happened.' Roy was soaked to the skin and even though he was a mate, I could see he was getting really pissed off. 'Come on Frog, we had better get these people out of the car.' The rain was getting worse and Roy was worried that the edge of the bank might give way. Roy was a very experienced village bobby and quickly took control of the potentially dangerous situation. He first called for assistance and then for the local garage owner, 'old Bert', to bring his crane lorry over. On the arrival of two more police cars the road at the bottom of the rise was closed both ways. The arrival of the Inspector from Stratford upon Avon Police Station added a certain seriousness to the situation. It was still pissing down with rain and the Inspector was well miffed to say the least. 'What on earth is going on here Tanner?' he addressed Roy, 'and those chaps in the car, are they all drunk?' (The lads had started to sing.) Quick as a flash, Roy (bless him) replied 'No, no, Inspector. They are just trying to keep their spirits up until we can get them out.' 'Well, man. Don't stand there looking. Get them out.' Roy looked at me and scowled.

In the meantime old Bert had arrived with his mobile crane. He was as pissed as a fart. He had been in the Three Tuns pub all night with us! 'What's his nibs doing here?' said Bert, referring to the Inspector. 'Shurrup Bert, I'm in trouble as it is.' Roy whispered. 'There are traffic jams a mile long both ways down there' said Bert. 'Look Bert, how can we secure the car so that we can get everybody out?' Roy was at a loss for ideas. 'Well, I can't get the crane up here. It's too narrow and anyway the ground's too wet and weak to take the weight.' Bert paused for a little while. 'The best I can do is to run a cable up the bank, run it round the big tree at the back, secure it into the car and try to winch it back onto hard ground.' Roy brightened up. 'That gives me an idea, Bert. While you're doing that I'll bring my Panda car up and we can rope the big car to it while we get them out.' 'Right-ho Roy.' Old Bert turned to go down to his crane and slipped on his arse in the mud. Roy just shook his head. 'Bloody hell, everybody's pissed here.'

Roy by this time was absolutely saturated. Like a good-un he drove the Panda car up the narrow lane, by this time ankle deep in mud. He instructed the folk in the car to gently open the door windows so that he could pass the rope around the centre door column and attach it to the axle of the Panda car. That having been done Roy then reversed the Panda to tighten the rope off. 'Open both doors lads and leave the car quickly. Don't make any moves backwards.'

A few moments later everyone was safely out of the car. Then the unthinkable happened. The great silver vehicle began to move and, as if in slow motion, the wheels were lifted off the ground. Nothing in this world was going to stop it going over the edge.

To my utter disbelief the Panda car was being dragged towards the edge of the drop. Then, a mighty grind and the car dropped like a stone. The Panda car was whipped like a rag doll. Ranch Wagon and Panda car went flying through the air onto the road below. Roy and I walked slowly to the edge. As we looked over we were both stunned speechless in disbelief. The Ranch Wagon was on its roof in the middle of the road and the Panda car (completely unrecognisable and still attached to the rope) was half way up the bank on the opposite side of the road. While all this was going on the ambulance had taken old Bert to hospital. Apparently he had caught his hand in a winch and broken his wrist.

As I gazed on to the scene I could see police car lights, orange and blue, flashing in the torrential rain. The incredible wreckage of twisted metal looked like a plane crash. Roy looked at me and said 'How the bloody hell am I going to write my report?' The Inspector broke the silence. 'Get this lot cleared up Tanner and I'll see you tomorrow.' 'Yes Inspector.' Poor Roy, what a night he had.

The Stratford Herald newspaper made a big thing of the incident. Roy was hailed a local hero, sacrificing his car and risking life and limb to save ten people from injury and possible death. 'LOCAL BOBBY AND POP STAR SAVE TEN PEOPLE FROM DISASTER'. Roy was commended by the Force and he got a new Panda! I had owned my Ranch Wagon estate for only nine days. It was now in the scrapyard.

I was exonerated from any blame. It was considered to be an accident caused by the extremely bad weather conditions. Old Bert was compensated for his injury and loss of work. He managed to string his disability out for eighteen months. Old Bert told the story of the car on the cliff to anyone who would listen in the Three Tuns pub, right up until the day he died.

Undaunted I decided to buy another car. I had heard that the BMW was a nice vehicle so H. Cain took me to the showrooms in Birmingham.

I used to like going into the posh showrooms because the salesmen would look down their noses as we walked in. Two scruffy looking gits wandering round their expensive motors, opening the doors and sitting in them; kicking the tyres and trying the horn - great fun.

Eventually a toffee nosed geezer would saunter up. 'Can I be of assistance?' His disdain was as plain as the nose on his face. 'How much are these mate?' A slight clearing of the throat. 'Thirty-five thousand pounds.' 'Is that all? Is that with all the extras?' 'These cars are built with all extras included.' 'Can I have this one then?' A short silence. 'Well certainly Sir.' All of a sudden we had become sirs. 'If Sir would like to come this way we can complete the necessary paperwork. After a three week wait the car would be delivered to my home.

The car was delivered on a Wednesday afternoon. It was metallic green with a black leather interior. An absolute work of engineering art. I drove this wonderful car to H. Cain's and then to the other members of my band's homes just to try it out and do a bit of posing.

Two weeks later we were invited to play for the Midland Bank's Equestrian Horse Show at White Horse Common Road in Solihull. Princess Anne would be competing and Guest of Honour at the evening 'do'.
I told H. Cain that I would go in my new car just to look a bit flash. My old friend smiled and agreed to meet me there.

I arrived without mishap and we played for half an hour before dinner. We were invited to join the rest of the party for the remainder of the evening. Those were the days before breathalyser tests were in force so, like us all, we would have a skinfull and as long as we felt we could drive, we would. Towards the end of the evening the crowd began to thin out. I had been chatting to the boss of the Equestrian Club when H. Cain said that the rest of the band were leaving. After a couple of more drinks with the gaffer I would be going home too.

As always in those days I was the very last to leave. I bade the jovial fellow good evening (it was about four in the morning) and left. I got into my beautiful new car and began my journey home.

Half a mile up the Club entrance drive, steady over the rounded ramps and out on to the White Horse Common Road.

Unfortunately there were road works in progress. I had noticed them on the way there but I had quite forgotten about them since. There were barriers and warnings but the vodka had diminished my vision somewhat and I was upon the excavation in a flash.

The streamlined nose of my BMW disappeared into the huge cavity in the road. The car then turned full turtle on its roof, wedged firmly and snug in the clay-pit

The hole was too narrow for me to open the doors so I was well and truly stuck upside down. The White Horse Common Road is a deserted highway so I would be there for the remainder of the night. I made myself as comfortable as is possible in this unfortunate position and, apart from the worrying smell of petrol, I was ok. The morning came and the noise of approaching workmen woke me up. 'There's somebody in here! Are you all right mate?' 'Yes, I'm fine. I just can't get out.' 'Hang on. We'll get help.' Shortly after the fire brigade arrived with the police. They burned the bottom out of the car after flooding the petrol tank with water. I was finally released soaking wet and freezing cold. 'How did you manage to get down there?' the officer enquired. 'I saw the roadworks but I was startled by a badger and lost control' I lied. 'Well, no damage done except for your car and that's a write off.' After a visit to hospital for a check up and to a police station to report the accident the police took me home. My BMW went to join Ranch Wagon in the scrapyard.

Foolishly I then decided to order an E Type Jag - a red one with chrome spoked wheels. I had to wait over six months for delivery and when it finally arrived I jumped into it and proceeded to drive it to Birmingham. Now, fortunately for me and the rest of the planet, I hate speed and have never driven a car at great momentum. Now I discovered that it is impossible to tootle along in an E type. The motor just took off with me holding on from grim death. I couldn't see over the bonnet and I had no control over it whatsoever. Having gone five miles in about three minutes I managed to stop the thing. I left it in a lay-by and caught the bus back home. On my return I informed the showroom of the location of the vehicle and requested them to collect it. I never saw it again and never want to.

Shortly after this the Range Rover came out and I immediately had a yearning to own one. When they first came on the market they were four thousand five hundred pounds each (a lot of money in those days). My old pal Roy Wood had just bought one and he told me they were great. He's very like me with cars. he told me how he took his Range Rover onto the beach at Weston Super Mare. He went for a drink and on his return the tide had come in and buried it! Another write-off.

I finally got the opportunity to get a Range Rover and, knowing my history, I decided to buy two of them. They only came in the one sand colour in those days so my two cars looked identical.

I had finally found a car that suited me. This car was virtually indestructible and absolutely 'Frog-proof'.

We were asked to perform a show at a university in Leeds. I suggested to H. Cain that we travel there in my new car. This would give me a chance to run it in. He agreed, and away we went. This superb motor was a joy to drive. It is a motorway driver's dream come true. We arrived in Leeds in early winter darkness. We were having trouble finding our destination through these dark, unfamiliar streets. We knew we were close and decided to ask directions.

A most agreeable young woman told me to keep going in the direction I was heading and there will be a small road on my left. 'Go down there and you can't miss it. Don't go fast because the street is only narrow and you might miss the turn.' I carried on on the main road keeping an eye open for a small secluded left turn. Suddenly there was a left turn. I swung the motor into it and found myself driving down three flights of stairs leading to the shopping precinct.

We bounced and rolled down and down until we hit the bottom. The vehicle lurched forward into the front of Woolworth's doors. Flying glass and bells ringing, with the sickening tear of ruptured timber. The precinct was deserted, so I quickly reversed the undamaged Range Rover out of the store and drove it straight back up the stairway. We finally found the venue and completed our show. Whoever discovered the damaged store must to this very day be at a loss as to what caused it.

I still had my Daimler but I only used it for posh occasions. one day I was invited to judge a Miss Birmingham Beauty Contest at Abigails Club in Birmingham City. This place was a very high class businessmen's club owned by my good friend Eddie Fewtrell. On your arrival fellows in waistcoats and bow ties would park your car and bring it back to you on your departure. I decided to go in the Daimler. This turned out to be a fantastic night out with plenty of booze and good company. I have to admit that I was totally pissed when I left. I decided, as all drunk people do, that I was well enough to drive.

I began heading home towards Stratford Upon Avon at three o'clock in the morning. Ten minutes later I was stopped by the police. 'Would you step out of the car Sir?'
'Certainly.'
'Is this your vehicle?'
'Yes.'
'Can you tell me the registration number?'
'No, I'm sorry I can never remember it.'
'What's your name?'
'Raymond Froggatt.'
'Raymond Froggatt? Bloody hell! My wife is your greatest fan.'
I thought 'Thank God for that!'
'Would you mind signing your autograph for her? She'll never believe me when I tell her.' I started getting cocky and said if you give me your address officer I'll send her a signed photo and album.' I was very pissed and was beginning to sway a bit. He wrote his wife's name and address and I was convinced I had pulled the wool over his eyes into thinking I was capable of driving.
'Where are you heading, Raymond?'
'To Stratford.'
'Well, you're on the wrong side of the town mate. This is the Pershore Road.'
'Oh yes, I'll cut across later on up road.'
'You'd better get off then.'
'Thanks a lot. Give my love to your lady.'
'I thought to myself, 'that's it, I've got away with it.' I got in my car as quick and as sober-looking as I could. As I shut the door, to my absolute dismay, I found I had got into the back. All I could see in front of me was a headrest! There were kiddy locks on the back doors. Just then I must have had a brain-storm, because instead of opening the windows to open the door from the outside, I decided to climb over the top of the seat. A sharp tap on the window. 'I've got to nick you haven't I Raymond?' He took my address and a note for me to produce my documents. I sent the

wife the album and photo as promised and I have never heard anything about the incident from that day to this.

The natural course of events with the movement of life, was to ensure that I was about the learn the hard way that old adage 'a fool and his money are soon parted'. I began to settle down to the serious business of taking care of business. I've learned that if you control yourself nothing on earth can control you. There is compromise in all things. The understanding of others becomes the understanding of yourself. If I know that I am right about something then I am immovable. I will never tolerate people whose intentions are to walk all over us, and I can smell a cheat a mile away. I am an easygoing man, and I will negotiate anything with anyone, but I won't suffer people who take me for a fool. People have fallen out with me because I refuse to run my business the way they think it should be run, and so benefit themselves. I say good riddance to them and that disassociation, for my part will last for ever.

The biggest disappointment in my life was to learn that people are not always what they pretend to be. In my days I have believed that if you are kind, then people will be kind back. I also believed that if you value someone then they will value you in return. I have found that this is not always so.

I am an idealist and a philantropist. Although I have been hurt many times by some people their attitudes have never been strong enough to throw me from that chain of thought. It's just that I'm more wary now and, like others, I share my love among fewer people these days.

Give understanding to the wicked and weak
Give open mind to troubled persons on the street
Behold the beauty in the earth beneath your feet
Behold uncertainty in love and all we seek
Be ever humble to the benefit of doubt
Be ever sensitive to the fire when it's out
Take heed of your temperament for such will harm you and tear
May God shelter thee in harmony, for harmony is care
Let us drink to the history of the power in the poor
Let us drink to the winter and the warmth of an open door
I give you the lonely, the weary and the child born simply free
The whole earth is turning as time turns you and me
We are never right, we are never wrong
We are only singers in life's song.

Chapter twenty five

H. CAIN

There could never be a single line of music or a common word from thought, whether cast from days of uncertainty or confidence of movement from the mind of me, that does not, somewhere, in the hope of it all, contain the influence of H. Cain.

Of all the men I've known in over fifty years of life, I am blessed with the true hand of circumstance, to be strengthened by the friendship of such a man.

Jon Cain's Birthday with Frog, H & Billy Paul.

The first time I saw him was at the auditions I told you about earlier. He was fifteen years old, sitting on a stool, playing a six string Rikenbacker guitar. Even though we were both very young I felt drawn to his personality and, in a deep, confused and youthful way, I knew imme-

diately that we would work together for a long time. That imagined 'long time' has turned out to be over thirty years and, if I'm lucky, it might last throughout the rest of my life.

We, together, have an inborn knowledge of each other's approach to music making. There can be few songwriters who can draw from the energy of absolute truth. For all of his strengths (and they are many) the honesty of this great musician stands above everyone I've ever known.

In the many changes, heartbreaks, set-backs and contempt thrown at us with impunity, never once has he put himself above the line of his fellows. H. Cain is a true giant of his industry and quite the greatest band man it is possible to be. His voluntary involvement in every aspect of the continuing existence of our band is absolutely inspiring and what in any way of a professional I have become has been solely due to his complete and unselfish existence in my professional and personal life. H. Cain believes in me, and such a compliment demands the very best of efforts to succeed.

Through all the years we have worked together I have seldom seen him rocked and disturbed by confrontation. His natural humour puts him above the stupidity of it all. I have learned that it is the snide, petty jibes that spring from jealousy delivered under the disguise of wit that will irritate him the most. A few people have made the mistake of colouring him with the brush of his quiet nature. I have to tell you now that all of them know how foolish a presumption that is.

It seems that H. Cain has always held a protective hand towards me and he has never stood by to watch me torn to pieces by spite.

I remember when we were kids we had to go to Yugoslavia to do an hour special concert for 'Television Belgrade'. Another noble venture in the great world of music business deals. In those days there existed a great band of musicians called 'The Peddlers'. Their manager - I think his name was Alan Smith - knew the television presenter 'Zora Kavich' of Belgrade Television. The deal was typical of the times. Our air fares would be paid for, also four days in the best hotel in Belgrade. We would perform an hour special TV show and the fee would go to Mr Smith. As always, we agreed. After all, it was great publicity for our name, so off we went.

Yugoslavia was then ruled by President Tito, and we have always respected the fact that Eastern European countries demand the same behaviour from foreign visitors as they expect, and get, from their own subjects.

We arrived in Yugoslavia, changed planes in Zagreb, and landed in Belgrade on a fine Monday afternoon. In all Eastern European countries the Custom's checks were a rigorous affair, especially for visiting musicians, but being musicians, we were used to being messed about.

All was well and we were met at the airport exit by the delightful Zora Kavich. The dear girl ushered us to a waiting bus and off we went to the best hotel in Belgrade.

The Hotel Belgrade was beautiful and the foyer was an orchestration of white and copper coloured marble. Huge three-feet diameter pillars and a gigantic marble staircase sweeping majestically to the highly polished terrazzo floor. Here and there the inanimate faces of huge statues gazed down on the black leather fifteen-feet-long couches, which accommodated the delightful rear ends of the occasional, very thought-provoking, high-class prostitutes.

Zora gave us some 'Dinar' (Yugoslavian currency) and told us to enjoy ourselves until she came to take us to the studio on Wednesday morning. We didn't know how much money we had got to spend but it looked like a lot, and we had until Thursday morning to spend it.

We checked in and Zora said goodbye. Before she left she gave us a card each with the instructions that if we happened to get lost, or get into trouble of any kind, we were to give the card to the police. 'Goodbye boys. Have a nice time! I'll see you on Wednesday.' 'Tarra Zora. See ya!'

We all went to our rooms to change. Half an hour later we were down in the reception area looking for the bar.

After a magnificent dinner we retired to the lounge. Surprisingly the meals and all of our drinks were on the bill, so we began to wonder what we could spend our money on.

We had travelled all day so we decided to get some shut-eye. After all, we had all day Tuesday and Tuesday night to have fun.

It was Tuesday morning. We all met in the restaurant for breakfast. While eating we discussed our plans for the day.

We walked around Belgrade and found people dashing here and there, strange-speaking children laughing and kicking cans. We are all so alike.

We did our first TV show and in the making of it H. Cain, (although still very young) began to show his complete controlled professionalism, that remained a revelation to me right up until the very day of writing this.

I have a true companion on every street that I walk on. There can be no doubt that, without him, our band and the music we make would not exist. H. Cain's contribution to every corner of this effort lives in the very heart of me.

The friendship of my good companion has no conditions attached. The light of it is simply free. My personal days are rich in all things, for my thoughts and movement flow within the breath and love of my dear friend and his family. I would simply not be living without them, just existing while singing to the sun.

So there you see fortune my dear ones. I've passed many people on this bright shiny road. I've walked in shadows and I have laughed beneath blue skies. Along the way I met a man who called me friend.

H & Lynn's Children at Home

Chapter twenty six

GOING IT ALONE

It's not difficult to take chances in this business. Especially if, like me, all of the doors in the main line recording world have closed on you. I have accepted that a major recording deal will never be offered to me again and that big promoters will only tour me on their terms. That is to say I would be working under their budget restrictions, and my ambitions would be governed by their monetary arithmetic. Everything would be second rate, and my power of professional demands would be nil.

So it remains that it is essential for us to do everything alone. With the experience of H. Cain and myself it is certain that we can do as good a job of handling our careers as anyone and if we fail, it will be our own fault.

I have found it very important to take our show to the highest platform, simply because I feel that the fans deserve to see us where the stars shine.

The greatest struggle in the entertainment business is your own acceptance of who you really are, where you are going and what you will do when you get there. If you do not get to the place you hoped for it is important that your soul be rested, for it is certain that you are as precious as the most successful star, because you tried. At least you did that.

Our tour was arranged and all of our beginnings are the same. So I say to you, however low you are professed to be by your critics, to your peers you are stars, each and every one of you.

Our first self-promoted theatre tour began and, for the first time in my professional career I felt the very real gut-churning apprehension of a poorly attended concert.

There is no measure to guide you in promoting shows. Even if your advance ticket sales are low there is always a possibility of walk-up sales (that is to say people who decide to buy their ticket on the night of the performance). You just have to be courageous and hope for the best.

I have known promoters who only continue with a project if the ticket sales have covered all of their outgoings weeks before the concert is to be performed. There are a thousand excuses for a promoter to cancel a

show. On the other hand, if an artiste is unable to perform for some reason or another he's the biggest bastard alive. This is just one of the phenomenon that we the artistes have to accept. It's sad, but it's just another cross we all have to bear.

I couldn't begin to tell you how many times I have worked and never got paid. It's an occupational hazard that all of us have learned to live with.

All in all, and after all has been said and done, the music industry is great to be involved with and the multitude of fans make everything worthwhile. There are cold winds blowing down every street and walkways stepped upon by all manner of dreamer. The doorways along the dusty kerbstones will sometimes hold a feast of human kindness, there to drape the cloak of warmth and love upon the shoulders of a crying soul. So mighty the love my dears shining full square into the face of God. The eyes of angels wing their way to light the moments of our darkest time.

For all the memories born of other things and love, I see beneath the coloured dress of nature a fitting picture that is humankind. Though brushed with a million tears, this way and that, so it is with bruised and shaking hands we go. For all our ragged edges torn, we swing in time with all things.

So far as it is possible for anyone to succeed without the help and enthusiasm of the industry I think it is fair to say that, with the love and affection of our loyal and many thousands of fans, we have reached a measure of quite remarkable existence. On the great wall of music making of all kinds we have signed our names.

Deeds great or small, in music or otherwise, cannot be erased by spiteful comment. Among the broken spirits, shipwrecked hopes and dreams, amid the rivers of tears cried by the desperate and lonely; alongside of the cut and scarred, felled by the vicious axe swung remorselessly by those of callous nature, there you find a million souls rested in the avenue of beautiful memories. I rest, constantly smiling, in that valley. And one of those souls is mine.

I shall write and sing until my time is done. I have no say in that. I don't know where the songs come from or why people love them. They are sent to me from who knows where. We, together, scatter them, and where they land is determined by the gentle wind blown by God. I am in love with the winding melodies of our world and I've never kissed a single one. When I am finally called to my last performance I shall leave this earth with the sound of million cheers echoing down the wild wind of a multitude of applauding hands. My heart will rest in the comfort of an endless company of naked souls, cast forth to my longing, to hold close through all eternity.

For all the meaning of the life I've lived, the tears and the moments, moved the fall of joy that rains on me. The pearls of water dance and scatter all around the place I stand. The small bright spot where love was born; where a singer - Raymond who? - sang a song.

- THE END -

ALBUM LIST

1	POLYDOR	1968	THE VOICE AND WRITINGS OF RAYMOND FROGGATT
2	BELL	1972	BLEACH
3	BELL	1973	HANDLE WITH CARE (NEVER ISSUED)
4	REPRISE	1974	ROGUES AND THIEVES
5	REPRISE	1974	THE R.F. BAND (AMERICAN ISSUE OF ROGUES AND THIEVES)
6	BBC TS	1974	IN CONCERT PROGRAM - HIPPODROME GOLDERS GREEN
7	JET	1975	LET THE MEMPHIS MOON SHINE ON ME (NEVER ISSUED)
8	JET	1978	SOUTHERN FRIED FROG
9	JET	1979	CONVERSATIONS (AMERICAN ISSUE OF SOUTHERN FRIED FROG)
10	JET	1979	WARM AND SPECIAL LOVE (AMERICAN ISSUE OF SOUTHERN FRIED FROG)
11	JET	1978	ALL BECAUSE OF YOU (AMERICAN ISSUE OF SOUTHERN FRIED FROG)
12	M.C.	1980	STAY WITH ME
13	TOAD	1982	SOONER OR LATER (DOUBLE ALBUM)
14	HAPPY FACE	1984	WHY?
15	TOPAS	1988	IS IT ROLLIN BOB
16	RED BALLOON	1991	HERE'S TO EVERYONE - CD

THE RAYMOND FROGGATT CASSETTE LIST

1	SOUTHERN FRIED FROG
2	IS IT ROLLIN BOB
3	FROGGIE'S COLLECTION
4	RAYMOND FROGGATT (1986)
5	LIVE AT BIRMINGHAM ODEON 1987
6	TOUR 89
7	BIRMINGHAM TOWN HALL PART 1
8	BIRMINGHAM TOWN HALL PART 2
9	FROGGIE'S FAVOURITES
10	SOONER OR LATER (REISSUED)
11	WHY

ALSO NOTE A SERIES OF 8 CASSETTES WERE PRODUCED CONSISTING OF THESE ALBUMS:

VOICE AND WRITINGS
BLEACH
ROGUES AND THIEVES
WHY
SOUTHERN FRIED FROG
SOONER OR LATER
STAY WITH ME

ALSO A CASSETTE SINGLE OF MILLION MILES AWAY HAS BEEN ISSUED
THE RAYMOND FROGGATT SINGLES LIST

1	POLYDOR		HOUSE OF LORDS
	1967	56164	MAGIC CARPET (THE MONOPOLY)
2	POLYDOR		WE'RE ALL GOING TO THE SEASIDE
	1968	56188	IT ISN'T EASY (THE MONOPOLY)
3	POLYDOR		CALLOW LA VITA
	1968	56249	LOST AUTUMN (RAYMOND FROGGATT)
4	POLYDOR		JUST A LITTLE BIT OF LOVE
	1968	56274	ABC GOLDFISH (RAYMOND FROGGATT)
5	POLYDOR		THE RED BALLOON
	1968	56284	LOST AUTUMN (RAYMOND FROGGATT)
6	POLYDOR		ROLY
	1968	56294	TIME GOES BY (RAYMOND FROGGATT)
7	POLYDOR		ROLY
	1968	56294	ROSALYN (RAYMOND FROGGATT)
8	POLYDOR		MOVIN DOWN SOUTH
	1969	56334	IT'S ONLY ME (RAYMOND FROGGATT)
9	POLYDOR		HASN'T THE LORD BLESSED US
	1969	56358	LAZY JACK (RAYMOND FROGGATT)
10	POLYDOR		ANYTHING YOU WANT TO
	1969	56314	RING-TING-A-LING(RAYMOND FROGGATT)
11	POLYDOR		ANYTHING YOU WANT TO
	1969	59275	RING-TING-A-LING(RAYMOND FROGGATT)
12	POLYDOR		A MATTER OF PRIDE
	1970	2058-028	FISHER BOY (RAYMOND FROGGATT)
13	BELL		THE SINGER
	1971 BELL	1156	CHURCH FETE (RAYMOND FROGGATT)
14	BELL		RACHEL
	1972 BELL	1261	KENTUCKY SUE (RAYMOND FROGGATT)
15	BELL		RUNNING WATER
	1972 BELL	1261	ROCK N ROLL SONG (RAYMOND FROGGATT)

16	REPRISE RECORDS 1974 K 14328	ROADSHOW SALT (THE RAYMOND FROGGATT BAND)
17	JET RECORDS 1975 JET 749	TRY TO GET YOU INTO MY LIFE THIS COULD LAST ALL NIGHT (THE RAYMOND FROGGATT BAND)
18	JET RECORDS 1978 SJET 111	GIVE ME A CALL WARM AND SPECIAL LOVE (RAYMOND FROGGATT)
19	JET RECORDS 1978 JET 119	ME AND MY IDEAS LUCIE MAY (RAYMOND FROGGATT)
20	JET RECORDS 1980 JET 181	IT DOESN'T MATTER KELLY (RAYMOND FROGGATT)
21	ASTRA 1983 ESM 405	DON'T LET ME CRY AGAIN MAGIC CARPET (RAYMOND FROGGATT)
22	RATPACK RECORDS 1986 RPC 004	DON'T LET ME CRY AGAIN JETTING (RAYMOND FROGGATT)
23	RED BALLOON 1990 RB 0001	MAYBE THE ANGELS MAYBE THE ANGELS (INST) (RAYMOND FROGGATT)

ABC GOLDFISH	CA P P	FROGGATT RAYMOND WILLIAM MORRIS EDWIN H AND CO LTD CHAPPELL MORRIS LTD	034289480 039721179 058347753
ALL BECAUSE OF YOU	CA P	FROGGATT RAYMOND WILLIAM AQUARIUS MUSIC LTD ROBBINS MUSIC CORP LTD	034289480 046648166 026222419
ALWAYS GOODBYE	CA P	FROGGATT RAYMOND WILLIAM CHAPPELL MORRIS LTD	034289480 087047753

ANOTHER MAGIC MOMENT	CA CA P	FROGGATT RAYMOND WILLIAM BAILEY DAVID PHILIP MS	034289480 046909654
ANYTHING YOU WANT TO	CA P	FROGGATT RAYMOND WILLIAM CHAPPELL MORRIS LTD	034289480 087047753
ARE YOU ONLY FOOLING ME	CA P N	FROGGATT RAYMOND WILLIAM EDWIN H MORRIS CO LTD (GB) CHAPPELL MORRIS LTD	034289480 087518051 058347753
BAND MAN	CA P P	FROGGATT RAYMOND WILLIAM AQUARIUS MUSIC LTD ROBBINS MUSIC CORP LTD	034289480 046648166 026222419
BIG SHIP	CA P	FROGGATT RAYMOND WILLIAM CHAPPELL MORRIS LTD	034289480 087047753
BINDING ME LIKE A CHAIN	CA CA P	FROGGATT RAYMOND WILLIAM BAILEY DAVID PHILIP MS	034289480 046909654
CATHY	CA P N	FROGGATT RAYMOND WILLIAM EDWIN H MORRIS CO LTD (GB) CHAPPELL MORRIS LTD	034289480 087518051 087047753
COLD AS A LANDLORDS HEART	CA P P	FROGGATT RAYMOND WILLIAM AQUARIUS MUSIC LTD ROBBINS MUSIC CORP LTD	034289480 046648166 026222419
CHARLIE		MAUTOGLADE MUSIC LTD FROGGATT AND CAIN	
COME AND STAY WITH ME	CA P	FROGGATT RAYMOND WILLIAM FROGGATT MUSICAL ENTERPRISES	034289480 122202247
COMING ROUND	CA P N	FROGGATT RAYMOND WILLIAM CHAPPELL MORRIS LTD WARNER CHAPPELL MUSIC INTL	034289480 087047753 160654188
CONVERSATIONS	CA P P	FROGGATT RAYMOND WILLIAM AQUARIUS MUSIC LTD ROBBINS MUSIC CORP LTD	03428948 046648166 026222419

CORRINA	CA	TRAD	
	R	FROGGATT RAYMOND WILLIAM	034289480
	P	CHAPPELL MORRIS LTD	087047753

| COTTON BILL | CA | FROGGATT RAYMOND WILLIAM | 034289480 |
| | P | MS | |

DEAR FRIEND	CA	FROGGATT RAYMOND WILLIAM	034289480
	P	AQUARIUS MUSIC LTD	046648166
	P	ROBBINS MUSIC CORP LTD	026222419

DOG LAUGHED	CA	FROGGATT RAYMOND WILLIAM	034289480
	P	EDWIN H MORRIS CO LTD (GB)	087518051
	N	CHAPPELL MORRIS LTD	087047753

OTHER TITLES : CHURCH FETE

| DO I REALLY HAVE A FRIEND | CA | FROGGATT RAYMOND WILLIAM | 034289480 |
| | P | MURRAY MUSIC | 161767458 |

| DON'T LET ME CRY AGAIN | CA | FROGGATT RAYMOND WILLIAM | 034289480 |
| | P | MAUTOGLADE MUSIC LTD | 071628477 |

EDUCATION	CA	FROGGATT RAYMOND WILLIAM	034289480
	P	AQUARIUS MUSIC LTD	046648166
	P	ROBBINS MUSIC CORP LTD	026222419

| EVERYBODY'S LOSING | CA | FROGGATT RAYMOND WILLIAM | 034289480 |
| | P | MURRAY MUSIC | 161767458 |

OTHER TITLES : EVERYBODY IS LOSING

FELIX GUNN	CA	FROGGATT RAYMOND WILLIAM	034289480
	P	EDWIN H MORRIS CO LTD (GB)	087518051
	N	CHAPPELL MORRIS LTD	087047753

FESTIVAL OF FOOLS	CA	FROGGATT RAYMOND WILLIAM	034289480
	P	AQUARIUS MUSIC LTD	046648166
	P	ROBBINS MUSIC CORP LTD	026222419

FIRE DANCE SEQUENCE	CA P P	FROGGATT RAYMOND WILLIAM AQUARIUS MUSIC LTD ROBBINS MUSIC CORP LTD	034289480 046648166 026222419
FISHER BOY	CA P N	FROGGATT RAYMOND WILLIAM MORRIS EDWIN H AND CO LTD CHAPPELL MORRIS LTD	034289480 039721179 087047753
FLYIN	C A P	MILLAR WILLIAM KEITH FROGGATT RAYMOND WILLIAM AQUARIUS MUSIC LTD	070166005 034289480 046648166
FOLLOW YOU	CA P	FROGGATT RAYMOND WILLIAM MS	034289480
FOOLISH PEOPLE	CA P N	FROGGATT RAYMOND WILLIAM CHAPPELL & CO LTD (LONDON WARNER CHAPPELL MUSIC INTL	034289480 087047753 160654188
FOOLS RUSH IN	CA P P	FROGGATT RAYMOND WILLIAM AQUARIUS MUSIC LTD ROBBINS MUSIC CORP LTD	034289480 046648166 026222419
FOR YOU AND FOR ME	CA P P	FROGGATT RAYMOND WILLIAM AQUARIUS MUSIC LTD ROBBINS MUSIC CORP LTD	034289480 046648166 026222419
FRENCH PAINTER	CA P P	FROGGATT RAYMOND WILLIAM AQUARIUS MUSIC LTD ROBBINS MUSIC CORP LTD	034289480 046648166 026222419
FROGGATT WENT ACA TRAD COURTIN R	 P N	FROGGATT RAYMOND WILLIAM EDWIN H MORRIS CO LTD (GB) CHAPPELL MORRIS LTD	034289480 087518051 058347753
GEORGIA PINES	CA P P	FROGGATT RAYMOND WILLIAM AQUARIUS MUSIC LTD ROBBINS MUSIC CORP LTD	034289480 046648166 026222419
GET ON BOARD	CA P P	FROGGATT RAYMOND WILLIAM CHAPPELL & CO LTD (LONDON) WARNER CHAPPELL MUSIC INTL	034289480 005876674 160654188

GIVE ME A CALL	CA	FROGGATT RAYMOND WILLIAM	034289480
	P	AQUARIUS MUSIC LTD	046648166
	N	ROBBINS MUSIC CORP LTD	026222419
GOIN' AWAY	CA	FROGGATT RAYMOND WILLIAM	034289480
	P	CHAPPELL MORRIS LTD	058347753
GOING TO THE ZOO	CA	FROGGATT RAYMOND WILLIAM	034289480
	P	MORRIS EDWIN H AND CO LTD	039721179
	N	CHAPPELL MORRIS LTD	058347753
GOIN' HOME	CA	FROGGATT RAYMOND WILLIAM	034289480
	P	EDWIN H MORRIS CO LTD (GB)	087518051
	N	CHAPPELL MORRIS LTD	058347753
GOODBYE IN A LETTER	CA	FROGGATT RAYMOND WILLIAM	034289480
	P	AQUARIUS MUSIC LTD	046648166
	P	ROBBINS MUSIC CORP LTD	026222419
GUN	CA	FROGGATT RAYMOND WILLIAM	034289480
	P	AQUARIUS MUSIC LTD	046648166
	N	ROBBINS MUSIC CORP LTD	026222419
HANDS OUT	CA	FROGGATT RAYMOND WILLIAM	034289480
	P	CHAPPELL & CO LTD (LONDON)	005876674
	N	WARNER CHAPPELL MUSIC INTL	160654188
HASN'T THE LORD BLESSED US	CA	FROGGATT RAYMOND WILLIAM	034289480
	P	CHAPPELL MORRIS LTD	058347753
HAVE YOU SEEN THE CHILDREN	CA	FROGGATT RAYMOND WILLIAM	034289480
	P	CHAPPELL INTL MUSIC PUD	046954747
	N	WARNER CHAPPELL MUSIC INTL	160654188
HEATHER	CA	FROGGATT RAYMOND WILLIAM	034289480
	P	MURRAY MUSIC	161767458

OTHER TITLES : I'LL GATHER HEATHER

HERE'S TO BUTTERFLIES	CA	FROGGATT RAYMOND WILLIAM	034289480
	P	CHAPPELL MORRIS LTD	058347753
	N	WARNER CHAPPELL MUSIC INTL	160654188

HOW THE EAGLES FLY	CA CA P	FROGGATT RAYMOND WILLIAM LAWTON IAN MS	034289480
HURRICANE	CA CA	FROGGATT RAYMOND WILLIAM FROGGATT MUSICAL ENTERPRISES	034289480 122202247
I'LL ALWAYS SEND YOU FLOWERS	CA P	FROGGATT RAYMOND WILLIAM MURRAY MUSIC	034289480 161767458

OTHER TITLES : YOU ALWAYS SEND ME FLOWERS

ICY WINDS	CA P N	FROGGATT RAYMOND WILLIAM MORRIS EDWIN H AND CO LTD CHAPPELL MORRIS LTD	034289480 039721179 058347753
I DIDN'T BELIEVE MY EYES	CA P N	FROGGATT RAYMOND WILLIAM CHAPPELL MORRIS LTD WARNER CHAPPELL MUSIC INTL	034289480 058347753 160654188
I DON'T KNOW	CA P	FROGGATT RAYMOND WILLIAM MURRAY MUSIC	034289480 161767458
I DREAM OF HOME	CA P P	FROGGATT RAYMOND WILLIAM AQUARIUS MUSIC LTD ROBBINS MUSIC CORP LTD	034289480 046648166 026222419
I FALL APART AGAIN	CA P	FROGGATT RAYMOND WILLIAM MURRAY MUSIC	034289480 161767458
I JUST GIVE HER MY LOVE	CA P N	FROGGATT RAYMOND WILLIAM CHAPPELL & CO LTD (LONDON) WARNER CHAPPELL MUSIC INTL	034289480 005876674 160654188
I'LL FOLLOW YOU	CA P P	FROGGATT RAYMOND WILLIAM AQUARIUS MUSIC LTD ROBBINS MUSIC CORP LTD	034289480 046648166 026222419

I'M GETTING TIRED	CA	FROGGATT RAYMOND WILLIAM	034289480
	P	CHAPPELL MORRIS LTD	058347753
	N	WARNER CHAPPELL MUSIC INTL	160654188

I'M SURE	CA	FROGGATT RAYMOND WILLIAM	034289480
	P	CHAPPELL & CO LTD (LONDON)	005876674
	N	WARNER CHAPPELL MUSIC INTL	160654188

| I'M YOURS | CA | FROGGATT RAYMOND WILLIAM | 034289480 |
| | P | MS | |

INSIDE OUT UPSIDE DOWN	CA	FROGGATT RAYMOND WILLIAM	034289480
	P	EDWIN H MORRIS CO LTD (GB)	087518051
	N	CHAPPELL MORRIS LTD	058347753

OTHER TITLES : ALL THE WORLD IS INSIDE OUT UPSIDE DOWN

IN TIME	CA	FROGGATT RAYMOND WILLIAM	034289480
	P	EDWIN H MORRIS CO LTD (GB)	087518051
	N	CHAPPELL MORRIS LTD	058347753

INVISIBLE CHAIN	CA	FROGGATT RAYMOND WILLIAM	034289480
	P	CHAPPELL & CO LTD (LONDON)	005876674
	N	WARNER CHAPPELL MUSIC INTL	160654188

OTHER TITLES : INVISIBLE CHAINS

IT DOESN'T MATTER	CA	FROGGATT RAYMOND WILLIAM	034289480
	P	AQUARIUS MUSIC LTD	046648166
	N	ROBBINS MUSIC CORP LTD	026222419

| IT'S ALL OVER | CA | FROGGATT RAYMOND WILLIAM | 034289480 |
| | P | MURRAY MUSIC | 161767458 |

IT'S ONLY ME	CA	FROGGATT RAYMOND WILLIAM	034289480
	P	MORRIS EDWIN H AND CO LTD	039721179
	N	CHAPPELL MORRIS LTD	058347753

ITS RAININ	CA	FROGGATT RAYMOND WILLIAM	034289480
	P	EDWIN H MORRIS CO LTD (GB)	087518051
	N	CHAPPELL MORRIS LTD	058347753

I WANT ACTION	CA	FROGGATT RAYMOND WILLIAM	034289480
	P	AQUARIUS MUSIC LTD	046648166
	P	ROBBINS MUSIC CORP LTD	026222419

I WANT TO SING	CA	FROGGATT RAYMOND WILLIAM	034289480
	P	CHAPPELL & CO LTD (LONDON)	005876674
	N	WARNER CHAPPELL MUSIC INTL	160654188

I WILL MISS YOU	CA	FROGGATT RAYMOND WILLIAM	034289480
	P	AQUARIUS MUSIC LTD	046648166
	P	ROBBINS MUSIC CORP LTD	026222419

I WILL SEE YOU AGAIN	CA	FROGGATT RAYMOND WILLIAM	034289480
	P	MURRAY MUSIC	161767458

I WILL STAY WITH YOU	CA	FROGGATT RAYMOND WILLIAM	034289480
	P	AQUARIUS MUSIC LTD	046648166
	P	ROBBINS MUSIC CORP LTD	026222419

I WONDER IF YOU'RE LONELY	CA	FROGGATT RAYMOND WILLIAM	034289480
	P	MURRAY MUSIC	161767458

JEANNIE WITH THE LIGHT BROWN HAIR	CA	TRAD	
	R	FROGGATT RAYMOND WILLIAM	034289480
	P	EDWIN H MORRIS CO LTD (GB)	087518051
	N	CHAPPELL MORRIS LTD	058347753

JETTIN	CA	FROGGATT RAYMOND WILLIAM	034289480
	P	MS	

JOHN LENNON	CA	FROGGATT RAYMOND WILLIAM	034289480
	P	MORRIS EDWIN H AND CO LTD	039721179
	N	CHAPPELL MORRIS LTD	058347753

JUST A LITTLE BIT OF LOVE	CA	FROGGATT RAYMOND WILLIAM	034289480
	P	EDWIN H MORRIS CO LTD (GB)	087518051
	N	CHAPPELL MORRIS LTD	058347753

JUST ANOTHER NIGHT	CA	FROGGATT RAYMOND WILLIAM	034289480
	P	CHAPPELL MORRIS LTD	058347753

KEEP ROWING	CA	FROGGATT RAYMOND WILLIAM	034289480
	P	MURRAY MUSIC	161767458
KELLY	CA	FROGGATT RAYMOND WILLIAM	034289480
	P	AQUARIUS MUSIC LTD	046648166
	P	ROBBINS MUSIC CORP LTD	026222419
KENTUCKY SUE	CA	FROGGATT RAYMOND WILLIAM	034289480
	P	CHAPPELL & CO LTD (LONDON)	005876674
	N	WARNER CHAPPELL MUSIC INTL	160654188
LADY'S STOLEN ME AWAY	CA	FROGGATT RAYMOND WILLIAM	034289480
	P	CHAPPELL & CO LTD (LONDON)	005876674
	N	WARNER CHAPPELL MUSIC INTL	160654188
LAY LAY ME DOWN	CA	FROGGATT RAYMOND WILLIAM	034289480
	P	MS	
LAZY JACK	CA	FROGGATT RAYMOND WILLIAM	034289480
	P	EDWIN H MORRIS CO LTD (GB)	087518051
	N	CHAPPELL MORRIS LTD	058347753
LET THE MOON SHINE ON ME	CA	FROGGATT RAYMOND WILLIAM	034289480
	P	AQUARIUS MUSIC LTD	046648166
	P	ROBBINS MUSIC CORP LTD	026222419
LIFE GOES ON THE SAME	CA	FROGGATT RAYMOND WILLIAM	034289480
	P	MURRAY MUSIC	161767458
LIKE A CANNON BALL	CA	FROGGATT RAYMOND WILLIAM	034289480
	P	AQUARIUS MUSIC LTD	046648166
	P	ROBBINS MUSIC CORP LTD	026222419

OTHER TITLES : I FEEL LIKE A CANNON BALL

LONDON BOUND	CA	FROGGATT RAYMOND WILLIAM	034289480
	P	AQUARIUS MUSIC LTD	046648166
	P	ROBBINS MUSIC CORP LTD	026222419
LONELY OLD WORLD	CA	FROGGATT RAYMOND WILLIAM	034289480
	P	CHAPPELL MORRIS LTD	058347753

LONELY WORLD	CA	FROGGATT RAYMOND WILLIAM	034289480
	P	EDWIN H MORRIS CO LTD (GB)	087518051
	N	CHAPPELL MORRIS LTD	058347753
LOOK FOR EVERY DAY	CA	FROGGATT RAYMOND WILLIAM	034289480
	P	AQUARIUS MUSIC LTD	046648166
	P	ROBBINS MUSIC CORP LTD	026222419
LOST AUTUMN	CA	FROGGATT RAYMOND WILLIAM	034289480
	P	CHAPPELL MORRIS LTD	058347753
LOUISE	CA	FROGGATT RAYMOND WILLIAM	034289480
	P	CHAPPELL MORRIS LTD	058347753
LUCI MAY	CA	FROGGATT RAYMOND WILLIAM	034289480
	P	MERVYN MUSIC	020582416
LUCY MAY	CA	FROGGATT RAYMOND WILLIAM	034289480
	P	AQUARIUS MUSIC LTD	046648166
	P	ROBBINS MUSIC CORP LTD	026222419
MAGIC CARPET	CA	FROGGATT RAYMOND WILLIAM	034289480
	P	MAUTOGLADE MUSIC LTD	071628477
MAGIC SHADOWS	CA	FROGGATT RAYMOND WILLIAM	034289480
	P	MURRAY MUSIC	161767458
MATTER OF PRIDE	CA	FROGGATT RAYMOND WILLIAM	034289480
	P	EDWIN H MORRIS CO LTD (GB)	087518051
	N	CHAPPELL MORRIS LTD	058347753
MAYBE THE ANGELS	CA	FROGGATT RAYMOND WILLIAM	034289480
	CA	HARTLEY CAIN STANLEY THOMAS	160331511
	P	MS	
MAYBE TODAY	CA	FROGGATT RAYMOND WILLIAM	034289480
		EDWIN H MORRIS CO LTD (GB)	087518051
	N	CHAPPELL MORRIS LTD	058347753
ME AND MY IDEAS	CA	FROGGATT RAYMOND WILLIAM	034289480
	P	AQUARIUS MUSIC LTD	046648166
	P	ROBBINS MUSIC CORP LTD	026222419

MILLION MILES AWAY	CA P N	FROGGATT RAYMOND WILLIAM MORRIS EDWIN H AND CO LTD CHAPPELL MORRIS LTD	034289480 039721179 058347753
MOONFLEET	CA P N	FROGGATT RAYMOND WILLIAM CHAPPELL & CO LTD (LONDON) WARNER CHAPPELL MUSIC INTL	034289480 005876674 160654188
MOONSHINE	CA P P	FROGGATT RAYMOND WILLIAM AQUARIUS MUSIC LTD ROBBINS MUSIC CORP LTD	034289480 046648166 026222419
MOVIN' DOWN SOUTH	CA P N	FROGGATT RAYMOND WILLIAM EDWIN H MORRIS CO LTD (GB) CHAPPELL MORRIS LTD	034289480 087518051 058347753
MY BACK YARD	CA P N	FROGGATT RAYMOND WILLIAM EDWIN H MORRIS CO LTD (GB) CHAPPELL MORRIS LTD	034289480 087518051 058347753
MY EYES HURT	CA P N	FROGGATT RAYMOND WILLIAM CHAPPELL & CO LTD (LONDON) WARNER CHAPPELL MUSIC INTL	034289480 005876674 160654188
MY LITTLE GIRL	CA P N	FROGGATT RAYMOND WILLIAM CHAPPELL & CO LTD (LONDON) WARNER CHAPPELL MUSIC INTL	034289480 05876674 160654188
MY WISH	CA P N	FROGGATT RAYMOND WILLIAM EDWIN H MORRIS CO LTD (GB) CHAPPELL MORRIS LTD	034289480 087518051 058347753
NOW WE HAVE EVERYTHING	CA P P	FROGGATT RAYMOND WILLIAM AQUARIUS MUSIC LTD ROBBINS MUSIC CORP LTD	034289480 046648166 026222419
OLD ACCORDION	CA P N	FROGGATT RAYMOND WILLIAM EDWIN H MORRIS CO LTD (GB) CHAPPELL MORRIS LTD	034289480 087518051 058347753
OLD DREAMS	CA P	FROGGATT RAYMOND WILLIAM MURRAY MUSIC	034289480 161767458

ONLY THE MEMORIES	CA	FROGGATT RAYMOND WILLIAM	034289480
	P	AQUARIUS MUSIC LTD	046648166
	P	ROBBINS MUSIC CORP LTD	026222419

| PART OF YOUR WORLD | CA | FROGGATT RAYMOND WILLIAM | 034289480 |
| | P | MURRAY MUSIC | 161767458 |

| PEACE | CA | FROGGATT RAYMOND WILLIAM | 034289480 |
| | P | MS | |

POEM	CA	FROGGATT RAYMOND WILLIAM	034289480
	P	CHAPPELL & CO LTD (LONDON)	005876674
	N	WARNER CHAPPELL MUSIC INTL	160654188

POOR MADAME	CA	FROGGATT RAYMOND WILLIAM	034289480
	P	EDWIN H MORRIS CO LTD (GB)	087518051
	N	CHAPPELL MORRIS LTD	058347753

PUT IT IN THE BOOK	CA	FROGGATT RAYMOND WILLIAM	034289480
	P	AQUARIUS MUSIC LTD	046648166
	P	ROBBINS MUSIC CORP LTD	026222419

| RACHEL | CA | FROGGATT RAYMOND WILLIAM | 034289480 |
| | P | CHAPPELL MORRIS LTD | 058347753 |

| RAINBOW EYES | CA | FROGGATT RAYMOND WILLIAM | 034289480 |
| | P | MURRAY MUSIC | 161767458 |

RED BALLOON	CA	FROGGATT RAYMOND WILLIAM	034289480
	P	MORRIS EDWIN H AND CO LTD	039721179
	N	CHAPPELL MORRIS LTD	058347753

RESTLESS TRAVELLER	CA	FROGGATT RAYMOND WILLIAM	034289480
	P	AQUARIUS MUSIC LTD	046648166
	P	ROBBINS MUSIC CORP LTD	026222419

RIBBONS AND BOWS	CA	FROGGATT RAYMOND WILLIAM	034289480
	P	EDWIN H MORRIS CO LTD (GB)	087518051
	N	CHAPPELL MORRIS LTD	058347753

RING TING A LING	CA	FROGGATT RAYMOND WILLIAM	034289480
	P	EDWIN H MORRIS CO LTD (GB)	087518051
	N	CHAPPELL MORRIS LTD	058347753

RIVERS AND MOUNTAINS	CA	FROGGATT RAYMOND WILLIAM	034289480
	P	AQUARIUS MUSIC LTD	046648166
	P	ROBBINS MUSIC CORP LTD	026222419
ROADSHOW	CA	FROGGATT RAYMOND WILLIAM	034289480
	P	AQUARIUS MUSIC LTD	046648166
	P	ROBBINS MUSIC CORP LTD	026222419
ROBBER	CA	FROGGATT RAYMOND WILLIAM	034289480
	P	EDWIN H MORRIS CO LTD (GB)	087518051
	N	CHAPPELL MORRIS LTD	058347753
ROCK AND ROLL SONG	CA	FROGGATT RAYMOND WILLIAM	034289480
	P	FROGGATT MUSICAL ENTERPRISES	122202247
ROGUES AND THIEVES	CA	FROGGATT RAYMOND WILLIAM	034289480
	P	AQUARIUS MUSIC LTD	046648166
	P	ROBBINS MUSIC CORP LTD	026222419
ROLY	CA	FROGGATT RAYMOND WILLIAM	034289480
	P	EDWIN H MORRIS CO LTD (GB)	087518051
	N	CHAPPELL MORRIS LTD	058347753
ROSALYN	CA	FROGGATT RAYMOND WILLIAM	034289480
	P	EDWIN H MORRIS CO LTD (GB)	087518051
	N	CHAPPELL MORRIS LTD	058347753
RUNNING WATER	CA	FROGGATT RAYMOND WILLIAM	034289480
	P	FROGGATT MUSICAL ENTERPRISES	122202247
SAIL AWAY	CA	FROGGATT RAYMOND WILLIAM	034289480
	CA	HARTLEY CAIN STANLEY THOMAS	160331511
	P	MURRAY MUSIC	
SALT	CA	FROGGATT RAYMOND WILLIAM	034289480
	P	AQUARIUS MUSIC LTD	046648166
	P	ROBBINS MUSIC CORP LTD	026222419
SEVEN LITTLE LADIES	CA	FROGGATT RAYMOND WILLIAM	034289480
	P	MURRAY MUSIC	161767458
SHEB A KER	CA	FROGGATT RAYMOND WILLIAM	034289480
	P	CHAPPELL & CO LTD (LONDON)	005876674
	N	WARNER CHAPPELL MUSIC INTL	160654188

SHIFTIN'	CA	FROGGATT RAYMOND WILLIAM	034289480
	P	CHAPPELL & CO LTD (LONDON)	005876674
	N	WARNER CHAPPELL MUSIC INTL	160654188
SHINEY	CA	FROGGATT RAYMOND WILLIAM	034289480
	P	CHAPPELL & CO LTD (LONDON)	005876674
	N	CHAPPELL MORRIS LTD	058347753
THE SINGER	CA	FROGGATT RAYMOND WILLIAM	034289480
	P	CHAPPELL INTERNATIONAL MUSIC	046954747
	N	WARNER CHAPPELL MUSIC INTL	160654188
SLOW DOWN	CA	FROGGATT RAYMOND WILLIAM	034289480
	P	MURRAY MUSIC	161767458
SMALL MEANING WHEN YOU BLEED	CA	FROGGATT RAYMOND WILLIAM	034289480
	P	FROGGATT MUSIC	
SMILE AND A SONG	CA	FROGGATT RAYMOND WILLIAM	034289480
	P	AQUARIUS MUSIC LTD	046648166
	P	ROBBINS MUSIC CORP LTD	026222419
SOMEBODY SING IT AGAIN	CA	FROGGATT RAYMOND WILLIAM	034289480
	P	EDWIN H MORRIS CO LTD (GB)	087518051
	N	CHAPPELL MORRIS LTD	058347753
SOMEONE LIKE YOU	CA	FROGGATT RAYMOND WILLIAM	034289480
	P	FROGGATT MUSIC	
SOMETHING GONE WRONG WITH MY BABY	CA	FROGGATT RAYMOND WILLIAM	034289480
	P	AQUARIUS MUSIC LTD	046648166
	P	ROBBINS MUSIC CORP LTD	026222419
SOMETHING IN BEING A GIRL	CA	FROGGATT RAYMOND WILLIAM	034289480
	P	AQUARIUS MUSIC LTD	
	P	ROBBINS MUSIC CORP LTD	026222419
SOMETHING'S GOIN ON	CA	FROGGATT RAYMOND WILLIAM	034289480
	P	CHAPPELL & CO LTD (LONDON)	005876674
	N	CHAPPELL MORRIS LTD	058347753
SOMETHING'S GONE WRONG WITH MY BABY	CA	FROGGATT RAYMOND WILLIAM	034289480
	P	AQUARIUS MUSIC LTD	046648166
	P	ROBBINS MUSIC CORP LTD	026222419

SOMETIMES I WONDER	CA P N	FROGGATT RAYMOND WILLIAM CHAPPELL & CO LTD (LONDON) CHAPPELL MORRIS LTD	034289480 005876674 058347753
SOMETIMES PEOPLE GET HURT	CA P P	FROGGATT RAYMOND WILLIAM AQUARIUS MUSIC LTD ROBBINS MUSIC CORP LTD	034289480 046648166 026222419
SOMEWHERE UNDER THE SUN	CA P	FROGGATT RAYMOND WILLIAM MURRAY MUSIC	034289480 161767458
SONNET BY HARTLEY CAIN	C C P N	FROGGATT RAYMOND WILLIAM CAIN HARTLEY MORRIS EDWIN H AND CO LTD CHAPPELL MORRIS LTD	034289480 039721179 058347753
SOONER OR LATER	CA P N	FROGGATT RAYMOND WILLIAM CHAPPELL & CO LTD (LONDON) WARNER CHAPPELL MUSIC INTL	034289480 005876674 160654188
SPIN A THOUGHT	CA P P	FROGGATT RAYMOND WILLIAM AQUARIUS MUSIC LTD ROBBINS MUSIC CORP LTD	034289480 046648166 026222419
STAGE	CA P P	FROGGATT RAYMOND WILLIAM AQUARIUS MUSIC LTD ROBBINS MUSIC CORP LTD	034289480 046648166 026222419

OTHER TITLES : WILL MUSICAL

STAR CROSSED PERSON	CA P N	FROGGATT RAYMOND WILLIAM CHAPPELL & CO LTD (LONDON) WARNER CHAPPELL MUSIC INTL	034289480 005876674 160654188
STAY WITH ME	CA P P	FROGGATT RAYMOND WILLIAM AQUARIUS MUSIC LTD ROBBINS MUSIC CORP LTD	034289480 046648166 026222419
STAY WITH YOU	CA P	FROGGATT RAYMOND WILLIAM MURRAY MUSIC	034289480 161767458

STEALIN' AWAY	CA	FROGGATT RAYMOND WILLIAM	034289480
	P	CHAPPELL & CO LTD (LONDON)	005876674
	N	WARNER CHAPPELL MUSIC INTL	160654188
STEWBALL	CA	TRAD	
	R	FROGGATT RAYMOND WILLIAM	034289480
	P	EDWIN H MORRIS CO LTD (GB)	087518051
	N	CHAPPELL MORRIS LTD	058347753
STONE MOUNTAIN	CA	FROGGATT RAYMOND WILLIAM	034289480
	P	CHAPPELL & CO LTD (LONDON)	005876674
	N	WARNER CHAPPELL MUSIC INTL	160654188
STRING BOX	CA	FROGGATT RAYMOND WILLIAM	034289480
	P	EDWIN H MORRIS CO LTD (GB)	087518051
	N	CHAPPELL MORRIS LTD	058347753
SUMMER WITH SUSAN	CA	FROGGATT RAYMOND WILLIAM	034289480
	P	EDWIN H MORRIS CO LTD (GB)	087518051
	N	CHAPPELL MORRIS LTD	058347753
SUNSHINE IN YOUR LIFE	CA	FROGGATT RAYMOND WILLIAM	034289480
	P	MS	
TEACH ME PA	CA	FROGGATT RAYMOND WILLIAM	034289480
	P	CHAPPELL & CO LTD (LONDON)	005876674
	N	WARNER CHAPPELL MUSIC INTL	160654188
THAT'S WHAT YOU ARE	CA	FROGGATT RAYMOND WILLIAM	034289480
	P	CHAPPELL INTERNATIONAL MUSIC	046954747
	N	WARNER CHAPPELL MUSIC INTL	160654188
THEY CALL YOU RUNAWAY	CA	FROGGATT RAYMOND WILLIAM	034289480
	N	MURRAY MUSIC	161767458
THIS COULD LAST ALL NIGHT	CA	FROGGATT RAYMOND WILLIAM	034289480
	P	AQUARIUS MUSIC LTD	046648166
	P	ROBBINS MUSIC CORP LTD	026222419
THIS LORD'S CHILD	CA	FROGGATT RAYMOND WILLIAM	034289480
	P	CHAPPELL INTERNATIONAL MUSIC	046954747
	N	WARNER CHAPPELL MUSIC INTL	160654188

THIS MUST BE THE ROAD	CA P N	FROGGATT RAYMOND WILLIAM EDWIN H MORRIS CO LTD (GB) CHAPPELL MORRIS LTD	034289480 087518051 058347753
THREE O`CLOCK IN THE MORNIN`	CA P	FROGGATT RAYMOND WILLIAM MURRAY MUSIC	034289480 161767458
TIME GOES BY	CA P N	FROGGATT RAYMOND WILLIAM MORRIS EDWIN H AND CO LTD CHAPPELL MORRIS LTD	034289480 039721179 058347753
TOP OF THE STAIRS	CA P P	FROGGATT RAYMOND WILLIAM AQUARIUS MUSIC LTD ROBBINS MUSIC CORP LTD	034289480 046648166 026222419
TO SEE YOU GO	CA P	FROGGATT RAYMOND WILLIAM MS	034289480
TRAVELLIN` DOME ALL RIGHT	CA P N	FROGGATT RAYMOND WILLIAM MORRIS EDWIN H AND CO LTD CHAPPELL MORRIS LTD	034289480 039721179 58347753
TRAVELLIN`	CA P N	FROGGATT RAYMOND WILLIAM EDWIN H MORRIS CO LTD (GB) CHAPPELL MORRIS LTD	034289480 087518051 058347753
TRYIN SOMETHING NEW	CA P N	FROGGATT RAYMOND WILLIAM EDWIN H MORRIS CO LTD (GB) CHAPPELL MORRIS LTD	034289480 087518051 058347753
TRY TO GET YOU INTO MY LIFE	CA P P	FROGGATT RAYMOND WILLIAM AQUARIUS MUSIC LTD ROBBINS MUSIC CORP LTD	034289480 046648166 026222419
TURNPIKE	CA P N	FROGGATT RAYMOND WILLIAM CHAPPELL & CO LTD (LONDON) WARNER CHAPPELL MUSIC INTL	034289480 005876674 160654188
UNCLOUDED SUNSHINE	CA P N	FROGGATT RAYMOND WILLIAM EDWIN H MORRIS CO LTD (GB) CHAPPELL MORRIS LTD	034289480 087518051 058347753
UP IN THE AIR	CA P N	FROGGATT RAYMOND WILLIAM CHAPPELL & CO LTD (LONDON) WARNER CHAPPELL MUSIC INTL	034289480 005876674 160654188

VOICE OF	CA	FROGGATT RAYMOND WILLIAM	034289480
CHRISTMAS	P	MURRAY MUSIC	161767458
WARM AND	CA	FROGGATT RAYMOND WILLIAM	034289480
SPECIAL LOVE	P	AQUARIUS MUSIC LTD	046648166
	P	ROBBINS MUSIC CORP LTD	026222419
WATCHING	CA	FROGGATT RAYMOND WILLIAM	034289480
THE LIGHT	P	AQUARIUS MUSIC LTD	046648166
	P	ROBBINS MUSIC CORP LTD	026222419
WATCH YOUR	CA	FROGGATT RAYMOND WILLIAM	034289480
MOUTH	P	FROGGATT MUSIC	
WE'RE ALL	CA	FROGGATT RAYMOND WILLIAM	034289480
GOING TO THE	CA	ABLETHORPE LE	
SEASIDE	P	MORRIS EDWIN H AND CO LTD	039721179
	N	CHAPPELL MORRIS LTD	058347753
WERE YOU	CA	FROGGATT RAYMOND WILLIAM	034289480
ONLY FOOLING	P	EDWIN H MORRIS CO LTD (GB)	087518051
	N	CHAPPELL MORRIS LTD	058347753
WHAT I WANT	CA	FROGGATT RAYMOND WILLIAM	034289480
(YOU'RE WHAT	P	FROGGATT MUSICAL ENTERPRISES	122202247
I WANT)			
WHAT WILL I	CA	FROGGATT RAYMOND WILLIAM	034289480
DO NEXT	P	MORRIS EDWIN H AND CO LTD	039721179
	N	CHAPPELL MORRIS LTD	058347753
WHEN MY WORK	CA	FROGGATT RAYMOND WILLIAM	034289480
IS DONE	P	CHAPPELL & CO LTD (LONDON)	005876674
	N	WARNER CHAPPELL MUSIC INTL	160654188
WHEN YOU	CA	FROGGATT RAYMOND WILLIAM	034289480
FINALLY FALL	P	EDWIN H MORRIS CO LTD (GB)	087518051
	N	CHAPPELL MORRIS LTD	058347753
WHERE YOU	CA	FROGGATT RAYMOND WILLIAM	034289480
BIN' HIDIN'	P	CHAPPELL & CO LTD (LONDON)	005876674
	N	WARNER CHAPPELL MUSIC INTL	160654188

OTHER TITLES : WHERE YOU BEEN HIDING WHERE YOU BEEN HIDIN

WHITE PEARL HANDLE GUN	CA	FROGGATT RAYMOND WILLIAM	034289480
	P	AQUARIUS MUSIC LTD	046648166
	P	ROBBINS MUSIC CORP LTD	026222419
WHO CARES	CA	FROGGATT RAYMOND WILLIAM	034289480
	P	CHAPPELL & CO LTD (LONDON)	005876674
	N	WARNER CHAPPELL MUSIC INTL	160654188
WHY	CA	FROGGATT RAYMOND WILLIAM	034289480
	P	MS	
WILL	CA	FROGGATT RAYMOND WILLIAM	034289480
	P	AQUARIUS MUSIC LTD	046648166
	P	ROBBINS MUSIC CORP LTD	026222419
WIND RAIN AND SUN	CA	FROGGATT RAYMOND WILLIAM	034289480
	P	MORRIS EDWIN H AND CO LTD	039721179
	N	CHAPPELL MORRIS LTD	058347753
WINGS ON MY HEELS	CA	FROGGATT RAYMOND WILLIAM	034289480
	P	MURRAY MUSIC	161767458
WISE TO TURN	CA	FROGGATT RAYMOND WILLIAM	034289480
	P	AQUARIUS MUSIC LTD	046648166
	P	ROBBINS MUSIC CORP LTD	026222419
WISH GIVER	CA	FROGGATT RAYMOND WILLIAM	034289480
	P	CHAPPELL INTERNATIONAL MUSIC	046954747
	N	WARNER CHAPPELL MUSIC INTL	160654188
WITHOUT SALLY	CA	FROGGATT RAYMOND WILLIAM	034289480
	P	MURRAY MUSIC	161767458
WORLD'S UPSIDE DOWN	CA	FROGGATT RAYMOND WILLIAM	034289480
	P	MORRIS EDWIN H AND CO LTD	039721179
	N	CHAPPELL MORRIS LTD	058347753
WORRIES	CA	FROGGATT RAYMOND WILLIAM	034289480
	P	EDWIN H MORRIS CO LTD (GB)	087518051
	N	CHAPPELL MORRIS LTD	058347753
WOULDN'T HAVE MISSED YOU FOR THE WORLD	CA	FROGGATT RAYMOND WILLIAM	034289480
	P	MURRAY MUSIC	161767458

YOU OUTSIDE	CA	FROGGATT RAYMOND WILLIAM	034289480
	P	MORRIS EDWIN H AND CO LTD	039721179
	N	CHAPPELL MORRIS LTD	058347753
YOU SING SO BLUE	CA	FROGGATT RAYMOND WILLIAM	034289480
	P	AQUARIUS MUSIC LTD	046648166
	P	ROBBINS MUSIC CORP LTD	026222419
ZOO	CA	FROGGATT RAYMOND WILLIAM	034289480
	P	MORRIS EDWIN H AND CO LTD	039721179
	N	CHAPPELL MORRIS LTD	058347753